The Seagull Sar

✳

The Seagull Sartre Library

The Seagull Sartre Library

VOLUME 1

POST-WAR REFLECTIONS

JEAN-PAUL SARTRE

TRANSLATED BY
CHRIS TURNER

LONDON NEW YORK CALCUTTA

This work is published with the support of
Institut français en Inde – Embassy of France in India

✳

Seagull Books, 2021

Originally published in Jean-Paul Sartre, *Situations III*
© Éditions Gallimard, Paris, new edition, 2003

These essays were first published in English translation
by Seagull Books in *The Aftermath of War*, 2008
English translation © Christ Turner, 2008

ISBN 978 0 8574 2 904 9

British Library Cataloguing-in-Publication Data
A catalogue record for this book is available
from the British Library

Typeset by Seagull Books, Calcutta, India
Printed and bound in the USA by Integrated Books International

CONTENTS

*

THE REPUBLIC OF SILENCE

Never were we freer than under the German Occupation. We had lost all our rights, beginning with the right to speak. We were insulted to our faces every day and had to remain silent. We were deported en masse, as workers, Jews or political prisoners. Everywhere— on the walls, on the screens and in the newspapers— we came up against the vile, insipid picture of ourselves our oppressors wanted to present to us. Because of all this, we were free. Because the Nazi venom seeped into our very thoughts, every accurate thought was a triumph. Because an all-powerful police force tried to gag us, every word became precious as a declaration of principle. Because we were wanted men and women, every one of our acts was a solemn commitment. The often atrocious circumstances of our struggle made it possible, in a word, for us to live out that unbearable, heart-rending situation known as the human condition in a candid, unvarnished way. Exile, captivity and, especially, death, which in happier times we artfully conceal, became for us the perpetual objects of our concern; we learned that they were not inevitable accidents or even constant, external dangers, but must be regarded as our *lot*, our destiny, the profound source of our human reality. Every second, we lived to the full the meaning of that banal little phrase: 'Man is mortal!' And the choice each of us made of his life and being was an authentic choice, since it was made in the presence of death, since it could always have been expressed in the form: 'Better dead than . . .'. And I am not speaking here of the elite among us who were real Resistance fighters but of all the French people who, every hour of the night and day for four years, said 'No'. The very cruelty of the enemy drove us to the extremities of this condition by forcing us to ask ourselves questions we sidestep in peacetime. All those among us with any snippets of information about the Resistance—and what Frenchman was not at one point or another in that position—asked ourselves anxiously, 'If they torture me, shall I be able to hold out?' In this way, the very question of freedom was posed, and we were on the verge of the deepest knowledge human beings can have of themselves. For the secret of a human being is not his Oedipus complex or his inferiority complex. It is the very limit of his freedom, his ability to resist torture and death.

To those involved in underground activity, the conditions of their struggle afforded a new kind of experience. They did not fight openly like soldiers. They were hunted down in solitude, arrested in solitude, and it was in an abandoned, defenceless state that they resisted torture, alone and naked in the presence of clean-shaven, well-fed, smartly dressed torturers, who mocked their wretched flesh, and who, by their untroubled consciences and boundless sense of social strength, seemed fully to have right on their side. Yet, in the depths of this solitude, it was the others, all the others, they were protecting—all their Resistance comrades. A single word could have led to ten, or a hundred, arrests. Is not this total responsibility in total solitude the very revelation of our liberty? This abandonment, this solitude, this enormous risk—these were the same for everyone, for leaders and men alike. For those who carried messages without knowing what was in them and for those who directed the entire Resistance effort, the punishment was the same—imprisonment, deportation and death. In no army in the world is such an equality of risk shared by foot- soldier and generalissimo. And this is why the Resistance was a true democracy: for the soldier as for the commander, the same danger, the same responsibility, the same absolute freedom within discipline. Thus, in the shadows and in blood, the strongest of Republics was forged. Each of its citizens knew he had an obligation to all and that he had to rely on himself alone. Each, in the most total abandonment, fulfilled his role in history. Each, standing against the oppressors, made the effort to be himself irremediably. And by choosing himself in freedom, he chose freedom for all. This Republic without institutions, without army or police force, was something every French person had at every turn to conquer and assert against Nazism. We are now on the threshold of another Republic. Let us wish that this one will, in the full light of day, retain the austere virtues of that Republic of Silence and Night.

Lettres françaises (September 1944)

PARIS UNDER THE OCCUPATION

Arriving in Paris, many English people and Americans were amazed to find us less thin than they expected. They saw elegant dresses that looked brand-new, jackets which, from a distance, still seemed serviceable. Seldom did they encounter that paleness of face, that physical degradation that is, ordinarily, the mark of starvation. Solicitude, when thwarted, turns to rancour. I fear they rather bear us a grudge for not entirely conforming to the pathetic image they had formed of us in advance. Some of them, perhaps, secretly wondered whether the Occupation had been quite so terrible; whether France should not ultimately regard as a lucky break the defeat that had put it out of action and enabled it now to recover the status of a great power, without having earned it through great sacrifices. Perhaps they thought, like the *Daily Express*, that, by comparison with the British, the French had not had such a bad time of it in those four years.

It is to these people I would like to speak. I would like to explain to them that they are wrong, that the Occupation was a terrible ordeal, that it is not certain that France can recover from it and that there is not a single French person who has not on many occasions envied the fate of their British Allies. But as I begin, I can feel how very difficult my task is. I have known this same embarrassment once before. I was back from prisoner-of-war camp and being questioned about the lives of the prisoners: how was I to convey the atmosphere of the camps to people who hadn't been in them? With just a hint in one direction, all would seem doom and gloom; with a nudge in the other, all would look sweetness and light. The truth was not even 'halfway between the two'. It took a lot of inventiveness and skill to tell it, and a lot of goodwill and imagination to have it understood. I find myself faced with a similar problem today: how can I convey what Occupation was like to the residents of countries that remained free? There is an abyss between us and words cannot bridge it. When the French talk among themselves about the Germans, the Gestapo, the Resistance and the black market, they understand each other easily; but this is because they experienced the same things and they are filled with the same memories. The British and the French no longer have any shared memories; all that London lived through proudly, Paris lived out in despair and shame. We shall have to learn to speak of ourselves without passion; you will have to learn to understand our voices and grasp what, beyond words, can only be hinted at, and all that a gesture or a silence may mean.

Yet if I try to provide a glimpse of the truth, I run up against new difficulties: the Occupation of France was an immense social phenomenon concerning 35 million human beings. How can I speak for all of them? The little towns, the big industrial centres and the countryside met with different fates. Some villages never saw a German, while others had the occupying forces billeted on them for four years. Since I lived mainly in Paris, I shall confine myself to describing the Occupation in Paris. I shall leave aside the physical suffering, the hunger, which was genuine but hidden, our depressed vitality, the increased incidence of tuberculosis. After all, these woes, the extent of which will one day be revealed by the statistics, are not without their equivalent in Britain. Doubtless the standard of living remained appreciably higher over there than with us, but you had the bombing, the V1s and the military casualties; we were not fighting at all. But there are other ordeals. It is these I want to write about, I want to try to show how Parisians *experienced* the Occupation *emotionally*.

We must first rid ourselves of stereotypes: no, the Germans were not patrolling the streets with guns in their hands; no, they didn't force civilians to give way to them, pushing them off the pavements; they gave up their seats to old ladies in the Métro, they showed affection to children and stroked their cheeks; they had been told to act decently and they acted decently, with shyness and application, out of discipline; at times they even displayed a naive goodwill that found no outlet. And do not go imagining that the French showed them a crushing air of contempt. Admittedly, the immense majority of the French population abstained from all contact with the German army. But one should not forget that the Occupation was a *daily* affair. Someone who was asked what he had done under the Terror said, 'I lived . . .'. It is an answer we could all give today. For four years we lived, and the Germans lived too, in our midst, submerged, immersed in the unanimous life of the city. I could not help but smile at a photo from *La France Libre* that I was shown recently: a rough-necked, broad-shouldered German officer rifling through a tray of books on the banks of the Seine, under the cold, sad gaze of a little old bookseller sporting a very French goatee. The German has something of a swagger; he seems to be pushing his scrawny neighbour out of the frame. Beneath the image, a caption explains: 'The German defiles the banks of the Seine, once the province of poets and dreamers.' I entirely understand that the photograph is not faked but it is just a photograph, an arbitrary selection. The eye embraces a wider field: the photographer saw hundreds of French people rummaging through tens of trays and a single German, a small figure against this over-wide backdrop, a single German leafing through an old book. A dreamer, a poet perhaps—at any rate an inoffensive character. It is this entirely inoffensive aspect that the soldiers strolling through the streets presented to us the whole time.

The crowd parted before their uniforms and closed behind them, leaving a pale, unassuming—half-expected—patch of faded green among the dark clothing of the civilians. The same daily necessities caused us to rub up against them, the same collective currents tossed and stirred us together: we squeezed up against them in the Métro, bumped into them in the dark nights. We would no doubt have killed them without any compunction, if ordered to do so. We no doubt retained the memory of our grudges and hatred but these feelings had assumed a rather abstract air and, at length, a kind of shameful, indefinable solidarity had established itself between the Parisians and these troopers who were, in the end, so similar to the French soldiers. A solidarity accompanied by no sympathy but formed, rather, by a biological habituation.

At the beginning, the mere sight of them hurt us and then, gradually, we learned not to see them; they assumed an institutional character. What rounded off the sense of inoffensiveness for us was their ignorance of our language. A hundred times I heard Parisians speaking freely about politics in a cafe with a lonely German sitting just alongside, staring out blankly over a lemonade. They seemed more like furniture than people. When they stopped us, extremely politely, to ask the way—for most of us this was the only time we spoke to them—we felt more embarrassed than filled with hatred; all in all, *we were not natural*. We remembered the rule we had laid down for ourselves once and for all: never speak a word to them. But, at the same time, when faced with these lost soldiers, an old humanitarian helpfulness stirred in us, another rule that went back to our childhood, commanding us never to leave another human being in difficulty. Then we would decide, according to our mood or the occasion. We would say, 'I don't know' or 'Take the second left.' Either way, we went off feeling unhappy with ourselves. Once, on the Boulevard Saint-Germain, a military car overturned on top of a German colonel. I saw ten French people rush to pull him out. They hated the occupying forces, I'm sure; and among them, there would certainly be some who, two years later, were in the F. F. I., sniping along this same boulevard. But was this man lying crushed beneath his vehicle an occupier? And what were they to do? The concept of enemy is only entirely firm and clear when the enemy is separated from us by a wall of fire.

Yet there was an enemy—and the most detestable of enemies—but it had no face. Or at least those who saw it seldom returned to describe it. I would compare it to a tentacular monster. It seized upon our best men in the shadows and spirited them away. It seemed that people were silently gobbled up around us. You would phone a friend one day and the telephone would ring and ring in the empty apartment; you would ring his doorbell and he wouldn't come to the door; if the concierge broke in, you would find two chairs drawn up together in the hallway with German cigarette ends between the legs. When they had been present at the arrests, the wives and mothers of the disappeared would report that they had been taken away by very polite Germans, similar to those who asked for directions in the street. And when they went to enquire after them at avenue Foch or the rue des Saussaies, they were received with courtesy and sometimes came away with words of reassurance. In the avenue Foch, however, or the rue des Saussaies, howls of pain and terror were heard from the neighbouring buildings all day and late into the night. There was no one in Paris who had not had a relative or a friend arrested or sent to the camps or shot. There seemed to be hidden holes in the city and it seemed to empty itself through these holes, as though it had some undetectable internal haemorrhage. We did not talk about it much, in fact; we covered up this uninterrupted bloodletting even more than we did the hunger, partly out of caution and partly for reasons of dignity. We said, 'They've arrested him' and this 'they', similar to that used at times by madmen to name their fictitious persecutors, barely referred to human beings: it referred more to a kind of intangible, living tar that blackened everything, even the light.

At night we heard *them*. Around midnight, the isolated canterings of laggards resounded on the roadway as they tried to get home before the curfew, and then there was silence. And we knew that the only footsteps clattering outside were *theirs*. It is difficult to convey the impression this deserted city could give, this no-man's land pressed against our windows peopled by them alone. The houses were never entirely a defence. The Gestapo often made its arrests between midnight and 5 a.m. It seemed the door could open at any moment, letting in a cold blast of air, a little of the night and three affable Germans with revolvers. Even when we didn't name them, even when we were not thinking of them, their presence was among us. We felt it in the particular way objects had of being less our own; they were stranger, colder, more public, so to speak, as though a foreign gaze violated the privacy of our homes.

In the morning, we came upon innocent little Germans in the streets hurrying towards their offices, briefcases under their arms, looking more like uniformed lawyers than soldiers. In these familiar, expressionless faces we tried to find a little of the hateful ferocity we had imagined during the night. In vain. Yet the horror did not dissipate; and this was perhaps the most painful thing, this abstract horror that never quite settled itself on anyone. This was, in any event, the first aspect of the Occupation. Try to imagine, then, this perpetual coexistence of a phantom hatred and an over-familiar enemy whom one cannot quite come to hate.

This horror had many other causes. But, before we go further, let us avoid one misunderstanding: it should not be imagined as an overwhelming, keen emotion. I have already said: *we lived.* This means one could work, eat, chat, sleep and sometimes even laugh—even though laughter was quite rare. The horror seemed to be outside—in things. You could distract yourself from it for a moment, be excited by something you were reading, by a conversation, an affair, but you always came back to it; you realized it had not gone away. Calm and stable, almost discreet, it coloured our daydreams as it did our most practical thoughts. It was at once the weft of our consciousness and the meaning of the world. Today, when it has dissipated, we see it only as one element in our lives; but when we were immersed in it, it was so familiar that we took it sometimes for the natural tonality of our moods. Will I be understood if I say that it was intolerable and, at the same time, we got along with it very well?

Some madmen, they say, are obsessed by the feeling that an atrocious event has turned their lives upside down. And when they try to understand what gave them such a strong impression of a break between past and present, they can find nothing. Nothing had happened. This was roughly how it was with us. We felt at every moment that a link with the past had been broken. Traditions were interrupted, habits too. And we did not clearly grasp the sense of this change, which defeat itself did not entirely explain. Today I can see what it was: Paris was dead. There were no cars any more, no passers-by in the streets except at certain times in certain districts. We walked between stones; it seemed we were left behind from some mass exodus. A little provincial life had stuck to the corners of the capital; there remained the skeleton of a city, pompous and immobile, too long and too wide for us. The streets, which you could see down right into the far distance, were too wide; the distances were too great; the perspectives too vast: you lost yourself in them. The Parisians stayed at home or led their lives in the immediate locality, for fear of moving between these great severe palaces which were plunged, every evening, into absolute darkness.

Here again, we must avoid exaggeration: many of us loved the village-like tranquility, the dated charm that came over this battered capital in the moonlight; but that very pleasure was tinged with bitterness: what can be more bitter than to walk in *your own* street, around *your own* church, *your own* town-hall and taste the same melancholy joy as you do when you visit the Coliseum or the Parthenon by moonlight? There was nothing but ruins: shuttered, uninhabited houses in the sixteenth arrondissement, requisitioned hotels and cinemas, indicated by white barriers which you suddenly bumped up against, shops and bars closed for the duration, their owners sent to camps, dead or disappeared, plinths with no statues, parks partly barricaded off or disfigured by reinforced concrete pillboxes, and all these big dusty letters on the tops of the buildings, neon signs that no longer light up. In the shop windows you read advertisements that seemed engraved on tombstones: all-day *sauerkraut*, Viennese patisserie, weekends at Le Touquet, everything for the car.

But *we* had all that too, you will say. In London, too, you had the blackout and the restrictions. This I know very well. But these changes in your life did not have the same meaning as the changes in ours.

Though mutilated, though functioning on stand-by, London remained the capital of Britain. Paris was no longer the capital of France. All roads, all railways had led to Paris; the Parisian was at home at the centre of France, at the centre of the world. On the horizon of all his ambitions, of all his desires were New York, Madrid and London. Nourished by the Périgord, the Beauce, Alsace and the Atlantic fisheries, the capital was not, unlike ancient Rome, a parasitic city; it regulated the trade and the life of the Nation; it worked up the raw materials; it was the hub of France. With the Armistice, everything changed: the division of the country into two zones cut Paris off from the countryside; the coasts of Brittany and Normandy became forbidden zones; and a wall of concrete separated France from Britain and America. Europe remained, but Europe was a word that spelled horror; it meant servitude. The city of kings had lost even its political function, stripped of it by a phantom government at Vichy. France, divided by the Occupation into sealed provinces, had forgotten Paris.

The City was now merely a vast, flat, useless conglomeration, haunted by the memories of its greatness and sustained by intermittent injections. It owed its listless life to the number of goods wagons and lorries the Germans decided to let through each week. If Vichy sulked a little, if Laval made them twist his arm for Berlin's quota of French workers, the injections came to an immediate stop. Paris wilted and yawned with hunger beneath the empty sky. Cut off from the world, fed out of pity or by calculation, it had now merely an abstract, symbolic existence.

A thousand times in these last four years, French people have seen serried rows of bottles of Saint-Emilion or Meursault in the grocers' windows. On approaching, tantalized, they found a notice saying 'dummy display'. So it was with Paris: it was merely a dummy display. Everything was hollow and empty: the Louvre had no paintings, the Chamber no deputies, the Senate no senators and the lycée Montaigne no pupils. It was the purpose of the artificial existence the Germans maintained there—the theatrical performances, the horse-races, the miserable, lugubrious festivals—to show the world that France was intact because Paris was still alive. A strange consequence of centralization. The British, for their part, while flattening Lorient, Rouen or Nantes with their bombs, had decided to respect Paris. Thus, in this dying city, we enjoyed a symbolic, funereal calm. Around this islet of peace, iron and fire rained down; but, just as we were not permitted to share the labour of our provinces, we were no longer entitled to share their suffering. A symbol: this hard-working, quick-tempered city was now nothing but a symbol. We looked at each other and wondered whether we had not become symbols ourselves.

The fact is that, for four years our future had been stolen from us. We had to rely on the others. And for the others we were merely an *object*. Doubtless, the British press and radio showed us friendship. But we would have had to have been very presumptuous or very naive to believe that the British were pursuing this murderous war with the aim of freeing us. They were defending their vital interests, and doing so manfully, bearing arms, and we well knew that we entered into their calculations only as one factor among others. As for the Germans, they were contemplating the best way to incorporate this piece of land into the 'European' bloc. We could feel our destiny slipping away from us; France was like a pot of flowers that you put on the window ledge when it is sunny and bring in again at night without a 'by your leave'.

Everyone knows those sick individuals who are termed 'depersonalized', and who suddenly come to believe that all human beings are dead because they have stopped projecting their own futures forward and have, as a result, lost any sense of other peoples'. Perhaps the most painful thing was that all Parisians were depersonalized. Before the war, if we happened to look sympathetically on a child or young person, we did so because we sensed their future, because we obscurely divined it from their gestures and the lines on their faces. For a living human being is, above all, a project, an undertaking. But the Occupation stripped human beings of their futures. Never again did we gaze after a young couple, attempting to imagine their destiny: we had no more destiny than a nail or a doorknob. All our acts were provisional, their meaning confined to the day they were performed. Workers worked in the factories with no thought for the morrow: the next day there may be no electricity, the Germans may stop sending raw materials, they may decide suddenly to deport them to Bavaria or the Palatinate; students prepared for their exams, but who would have dared say with certainty that they could sit them?

We looked at each other and it seemed we were seeing the dead. This dehumanization and petrification was so intolerable that many, to escape it and regain a future, threw themselves into the Resistance. A strange future, barred by torture, prison and death, but a future we were at last producing with our own hands.[1] Yet Resistance was merely an individual solution and we always knew this: without it the British would still have won the war, with it they would still have lost it, if that was how it was meant to be. First and foremost, it had a symbolic value for us; and that

---

1 If one had to find an excuse, or at least an explanation, for 'collaboration', we should say that it too was an effort to give France a future.

is why many resisters were in despair: still just symbols. A symbolic rebellion in a symbolic city; only the tortures were real.

So we felt out of it. We were ashamed at not understanding this war that we were no longer fighting. We watched from afar as the British and Russians adapted to the German tactics, while continuing to ruminate on our defeat of 1940. It had been too quick and we had learned nothing from it. Those who congratulate us ironically on having escaped the war cannot imagine how ardently the French would have liked to take up arms again. Day after day we saw our towns and cities destroyed, our wealth obliterated; our young people wasted away; three million of us were rotting in Germany; the French birth rate was falling. What battle could have been more destructive? But these sacrifices, which we would have made willingly if they would have hastened our victory, had no meaning and were of no use except to the Germans. And this, perhaps, everyone will understand: what is terrible is not to suffer or die, but to suffer or die in vain.

In our absolute abandonment, we saw from time to time Allied planes flying overhead. Our situation was so paradoxical that the siren warned us of them as enemies. We were under strict orders: you had to leave your office, close your shop and go down to the shelters. We never obeyed: we stayed in the streets looking up into the sky. And this indiscipline should not be seen as empty revolt or a silly affectation of courage: we were desperately watching the only friends we still had. This young pilot in his plane above over our heads was connected to Britain, to America, by invisible bonds; it was an enormous free world that filled the sky. But the only messages he bore were messages of death.

You will never know what faith in our allies it took to continue to love them, *to want with them* the destruction they wrought on our soil, to hail their bombers, in spite of everything, as the face of Britain. If bombs missed their targets and fell on an urban area, we went to enormous lengths to find excuses; sometimes we even accused the Germans of dropping them, to turn us against Britain, or of deliberately sounding the alarm too late. I spent a few days at Le Havre with the family of one of my fellow POWs, during the spell of heavy bombing. The first evening we were gathered round the wireless, the father twiddling the buttons with a naive, touching solemnity; you would have thought he was celebrating mass. And, as the BBC gave us its first news, we heard a faraway roar of aircraft. We knew very well they were coming to drop their bombs on us. I shall not soon forget the mixture of terror and delight in the hushed tones of one of the women, as she said, 'Here come the British!' And for a quarter of an hour, without moving from their seats, to the sound of explosions all around, they listened to the voice of London; it seemed to them to be more present, and that the squadrons moving above our heads lent body to it.

But these acts of faith put us under perpetual tension: they often required us to suppress our indignation. We suppressed it when Lorient was razed to the ground, when the centre of Nantes was destroyed, when the heart of Rouen was hit. Perhaps you will divine the effort this took. Sometimes anger got the upper hand—and then we tried to reason things out, as you would over a passion. I remember, in July 1944, the train bringing me from Chantilly was machine-gunned. It was a harmless little suburban train; three planes passed overhead and in a matter of seconds there were three dead and twelve wounded in the front carriage. The passengers, standing on the track, watched as the stretchers went by, along with some green benches that had been brought from the platforms of the neighbouring station because there were not enough stretchers to carry all the bodies. They were white with anger and emotion. You were insulted, you were called inhuman and barbaric: 'Why do they have to attack a defenceless train? Isn't there enough for them to do across the Rhine? Let them go to Berlin! Don't like the anti-aircraft guns, do they?' and so on. Then, suddenly, someone found an explanation. 'Listen, normally they attack the engine and no one gets wounded. Only today the loco was at the back, so they shot at the front carriage. At the speed they were going, they didn't spot the change.' Immediately everyone fell silent. The people were relieved that the pilot had not committed an unforgiveable crime, because we could continue to love you. But this temptation to hate you was not the least of our misfortunes, and we often had to fight against it. And I can testify that on the days when we watched the smoke from the fires you had lit on the outskirts of the city, with the Germans, our conquerors, looking on sardonically, we felt totally alone.

Yet we did not dare complain: we had bad consciences. I first knew the secret shame that tormented us when I was a POW. The prisoners were unhappy, but they could not go so far as to pity themselves. 'Well,' they said, 'we're really going to cop it when we get home!' Their pain was keen and bitter; theirs was a disagreeable suffering, poisoned by the sense of having deserved it. They were ashamed before France. But France was ashamed before the world. It is pleasant to weep a little over your own fate. But how could we have found pity for ourselves when we were surrounded by other people's scorn. The Poles in my *Stalag* did not conceal their contempt; the Czechs condemned us for having abandoned them in [19]38; I heard a report of an escaped Russian, hidden by a gendarme in Anjou, who said of us, with a fond smile, 'The French? Rabbits! rabbits!'

You have not always been that gentle on us yourselves and I remember a particular speech by Marshal Smuts that we had to listen to in silence. After that, of course, we were tempted to cling to our humiliation, to wallow in it. Perhaps it would have been possible to defend ourselves. After all, the world's three greatest powers took four years to overcome Germany; was it not natural that we would give in at the first onslaught, having no one's help to withstand it? But it did not enter our minds to plead: the best of us joined the Resistance out of a need to redeem our country. The others remained hesitant and ill-at-ease; they ruminated on their inferiority complex. Do you not think this the worst of hardships—the one you suffer without being able to judge it undeserved or regard it as redemptive?

But just as we were going to give in to remorse, the Vichyites and collaborators, by attempting to push us in that direction, held us back. The Occupation was not just this constant presence of the conquerors in our towns and cities, it was also, on all the walls and in the newspapers, this vile image of ourselves they were trying to foist on us. The collaborators began by appealing to our good-heartedness. 'We are defeated,' they said, 'let's show that we're good losers:

let's acknowledge our failings.' And, immediately afterwards, 'Let's agree that the Frenchman is flippant, scatter-brained, boastful and selfish, he understands nothing of foreign nations and that the war caught our country falling to pieces.' Comic posters ridiculed our last hopes. Faced with so much baseness and such crude tricks, we stiffened; we wanted to be proud of ourselves. Alas, no sooner had we raised our heads than we rediscovered in ourselves our true grounds for remorse. And so we lived in the worst disarray, unhappy without daring to admit it to ourselves, ashamed and yet disgusted with our shame.

And, to cap it all, we could not take a step, eat or even breathe without colluding with the occupier. Before the war, the pacifists had explained on more than one occasion that an invaded country must refuse to fight and must exert passive resistance. This is easy to say. But, for that resistance to be effective, the railwayman would have had to refuse to drive his train, the farmer would have had to refuse to plough his field. The conqueror would perhaps have been inconvenienced, though he could bring supplies from his own country, but the Occupied nation would have been certain of perishing in its entirety in short order. We had to work, then; we had to keep up a semblance of economic organization for the nation, had to maintain, despite the looting and the destruction, a minimum living standard. Yet the slightest activity served the enemy, who had descended on us and stuck his leeches on our skin and lived in symbiosis with us. Not a drop of blood formed in our veins in which he did not share.

There has been much said of 'collaborators' and there were, admittedly, some genuine traitors among us: we are not ashamed of them; every nation has its dregs, that fringe of failures and the embittered who momentarily take advantage of disasters and revolutions. The existence of Quisling and Laval in a population is a *normal* phenomenon, like the suicide or the crime rate. But what seemed abnormal to us was the situation of the country, which was wholly collaborationist. The *maquisards*, who were our pride and joy, were not working for the enemy, but if the peasants wanted to feed them, they had to go on raising livestock, half of which went to Germany. Every one of our acts was ambiguous: we never knew whether to condemn ourselves totally or fully approve our actions; a subtle poison infected the best of undertakings.

I shall give just one example: the railwaymen, both the stokers and the drivers, were admirable. Their sangfroid, courage and, often, their self-sacrifice saved lives by the hundreds and enabled trains to reach Paris. For the most part, they were resisters and have proved it. Yet the zeal with which they defended our equipment served the German cause: these miraculously preserved locomotives could be requisitioned at the drop of a hat. Among the human lives they saved, you had to count those of the troops on their way to Le Havre or Cherbourg; and the trains bringing food supplies were also carrying war *matériel*. And so these men, who were concerned only to serve their compatriots, were, by force of circumstance, on the side of our enemies against our friends. And when Pétain stuck a medal on their chests, it was Germany that was decorating them. From one end of the war to the other, we did not *recognize* our acts; we were not able to claim their consequences as our own. Evil was everywhere; any choice was bad and yet we had to choose and we were responsible; every beat of our hearts drove us further into a horrifying state of guilt.

Perhaps we would have borne better the abject condition to which we were reduced if we had been able to achieve that unity against Vichy that Vichy constantly called for. But it is not true that misfortune unites. First of all, the Occupation scattered families to the four winds. A particular Paris industrialist, for example, had left his wife and daughter in the *zone libre* and—at least for the first two years—could not see them again or write them anything but postcards; his elder son was a prisoner in an *Oflag*, his younger son had joined de Gaulle. Paris was a city of absentees and the cult of memory we practised for four years was perhaps one of the more striking aspects of our situation; it was a cult directed, through our distant friends, to a sweetness of life and a pride in living that had now disappeared.

Despite our efforts, the memories paled more each day, the faces faded one by one. We talked a lot about the prisoners, then less, then even less than that. It was not that we stopped thinking about them but from having been precise, painful forms within us, they had become just gaping, empty spaces. Gradually they merged with the thinness of our blood; we missed them as we did fat, sugar or vitamins; in the same total, undifferentiated way. The taste of chocolate or *foie gras* vanished similarly, as did the memory of certain radiant days—of a 14 July at the Bastille, a walk with a loved one, an evening by the sea, or the greatness of France. And our exigencies diminished with our memories and, since one comes to terms with anything, we had the shame of coming to terms with our misery, with the swedes that were served at our tables, the tiny freedoms we still possessed, our inner emptiness. We simplified ourselves a little more each day and we ended up speaking only of food, less perhaps out of hunger or fear of the morrow and more because the pursuit of eating 'opportunities' was the only enterprise still within our scope.

And then the Occupation awakened old quarrels. It aggravated dissensions that divided French people. The splitting of France into northern and southern zones whipped up the old rivalry between Paris and the provinces again, between the North and the 'Midi'. The inhabitants of Clermont-Ferrand and Nice accused the Parisians of collusion with the enemy. The Parisians, for their part, criticized those in the *zone libre* for being 'soft' and for brazenly flaunting their selfish satisfaction at not being 'occupied'. From this point of view, it must be admitted, the Germans, by violating the clauses of the Armistice and extending the Occupation to the whole country, did us a great service: they restored the unity of the nation.

But many other conflicts persisted, such as that between town- and country-dwellers, for example. The peasants, wounded for many years by the contempt in which they believed they were held, took their revenge and held out on the city-dwellers: the latter, in return, accused them of supplying the black market and starving the urban population. The government stoked the quarrel with speeches in which the peasants were at times lauded to the skies and at others condemned for concealing their harvests. The brazenness of the luxury restaurants set the workers against the middle classes. In fact, these establishments were frequented mainly by Germans and a handful of 'collaborators', but their existence rendered social inequalities tangible.

Similarly, the working classes were only too aware that it was among them that forced labourers were recruited: the bourgeoisie was not, or was only barely, affected. Was this a German ploy to spread discord or was it not rather that manual workers were of greater use to Germany? I do not know. But, and this is a mark of our uncertainty, we did not know whether to rejoice that students largely escaped being deported or to wish, out of a sense of solidarity, that deportation would extend to all social strata. For the sake of com-pleteness, we must mention, lastly, that the defeat exacerbated the conflict between the generations. For four years, the soldiers of the '[19]14–18 war' blamed those of [19]40 for having lost the war and the soldiers of 1940, in return, blamed their elders for having lost the peace.

However, do not go imagining a France torn asunder. The truth is not so simple. These quarrels appeared mainly as obstacles to an immense, clumsy desire for union. Never perhaps was there so much goodwill. Young people dreamed obscurely of a new order; the employers were, overall, inclined to make concessions. Whenever two jostling Métro passengers came to blows, whenever a blundering pedestrian and a careless cyclist clashed, the same muttering went up from the crowd: 'How bad is that! French people quarrelling! And in front of Germans!' But, in most cases, the very circumstances of the Occupation, the barriers the Germans erected between us and the needs of clandestine struggle prevented these good intentions from finding an outlet. So these four years were a long, impotent dream of unity.

This is what lends the present moment its distressing urgency: the barriers have fallen, our fate is in our own hands. Which will win out—the old quarrels that have been reawakened or this great desire for solidarity? But from all of you watching from London, we must crave a little patience: the memory of the Occupation has not faded; we have barely awakened from it. In my case, when I come around a corner and see an American soldier, I react with a sudden, instinctive start: I take him for a German. Conversely, a German soldier, who had hidden in a cellar and wanted to surrender because he was starving, was able to ride unmolested down the Champs-Elysées on his bicycle a fortnight after the Liberation. The crowd had become so habituated that it did not *see* him. We need a lot of time to forget and tomorrow's France still has not shown its true face.

But we are asking you first to understand that the Occupation was often more terrible than the war. For in war everyone can perform his task as a human being whereas, in that ambiguous situation, we really could neither *act* nor even *think*. Unarguably, during this period—apart from the Resistance—France did not always furnish proof of its greatness. But you must first understand that active resistance was, of necessity, limited to a minority. And then it seems to me that this minority, which offered itself up for martyrdom determinedly and without hope, is amply sufficient to redeem our weaknesses. And, lastly, if these pages have helped you gauge what our country has suffered, in shame, horror and anger, I believe you will think, as I do, that even where it erred it is deserving of respect.

La France libre (London, 1945)

✳

WHAT IS A COLLABORATOR?

Crown Prince Olaf, who has just returned to Norway, estimates that 'collaborators' represent two per cent of the total population. Doubtless, the percentage was fairly similar in France. A survey of the various occupied countries would enable us to establish a kind of average percentage of collaborators in contemporary communities, since collaboration, like suicide or crime, is a normal phenomenon. But in peacetime, or during wars that do not end in disaster, these elements within the community remain in a state of latency. Since the determining factors are absent, 'the collaborator' does not reveal himself, either to others or to himself, but goes about his business; he may perhaps be patriotic for he is ignorant of the nature within him which, in favourable circumstances, will one day disclose itself.

During the present war, which made it possible to *isolate* collaboration in the way that illnesses are isolated, there was a parlour game popular among the British: the aim was to sift through all of London's prominent personalities and pick out which ones would have collaborated if Britain had been invaded. It was not such a silly game, since it came down to the idea that collaboration is a vocation. In fact, in our own country, there were no great surprises. You had only to know Déat[1] or Bonnard[2] before the war to find it natural that they should join forces with the victorious Germans. If it is true, then, that people do not collaborate by chance, but under the influence of certain social and psychological laws, it seems appropriate that we should define what is known as a collaborator.

It would be a mistake to confuse the collaborator with the fascist, even though every collaborator had, on principle, to accept the ideology of the Nazis. Indeed, some notorious fascists abstained from colluding with the enemy because they felt conditions were not right for the emergence of fascism in a weakened, occupied

1 Marcel Déat (1894–1955): French Socialist who drifted towards fascism, via what he termed 'neo-Socialism', in the late 1930s. In 1941, he founded the fascistic Rassemblement National Populaire (PPF). [Notes 2–19 are mine—Trans.]

2 Abel Bonnard (1883–1968): French Minister of Education under the Vichy regime and a member of the Académie française; was a Maurrassian who came to support Doriot's fascistic Parti Populaire Française.

France; former Cagoulards[3] went over to the Resistance. Conversely, a certain number of radicals, socialists and pacifists took the view that the Occupation was a lesser evil and they could get along with the Germans.

Similarly, we must be careful not to equate the collaborator with the conservative bourgeois. The bourgeoisie had, admittedly, been very half-hearted since Munich. They feared a war which, as Thierry Maulnier[4] clearly put it, would mark the triumph of the proletariat. This explains the negative attitude of certain reserve officers. But if the bourgeoisie made only a feeble effort in the war, it does not follow that they intended to surrender to Germany. All the workers and almost all the peasants were in the Resistance: most collaborators were, as a matter of fact, recruited from among the middle classes. But one should not jump to the conclusion that the bourgeoisie *as a class* favoured collaboration. To begin with, it provided many members of the Resistance: almost all the intellectuals, and

3 La Cagoule was the nickname of the so-called Organisation secrète d'action révolutionnaire, founded in 1935 by Eugène Deloncle. Its members, the *Cagoulards*, were united by fascistic leanings and a taste for political violence.

4 Real name Jacques Talagrand (1908–88). An intellectual who wrote on social and artistic matters for publications of the extreme Right.

a section of the industrialists and tradespeople, actively fought the occupying power.

If one were trying to define a strictly bourgeois standpoint, it would be more accurate to say that the conservative bourgeoisie was pro-Pétain and *attentiste*. It has been said that capitalism's interests are international and the French bourgeoisie would have profited by a German victory. But this is an abstract principle: in the event, what was at issue was the subordination, pure and simple, of the French economy to the German. The leading industrialists were not unaware that Germany's aim was to destroy France as an industrial power and, consequently, destroy French capitalism. And how could the French bourgeoisie, which has always seen national autonomy as synonymous with its own sovereignty as a ruling class, not have realized that collaboration, by making France a German satellite, was contributing to wrecking bourgeois sovereignty? While they were, most often, of bourgeois origin, the collaborators turned immediately against their class. For Déat or Luchaire,[5] the Gaullist was the prototype of the bourgeois who 'doesn't get it' because he cares about his wealth.

---

5 Jean Luchaire (1901–46): prominent collaborationist editor of *Les Nouveaux Temps.* Condemned to death for collaboration and executed.

In reality, collaboration is a phenomenon of disintegration; it was, in each case, an individual decision, not a class position. Initially, it represents a fixation by foreign collective forms of elements poorly assimilated by the indigenous community. It is in this respect that it is akin to criminality and suicide, which are also phenomena of disassimilation. Wherever social life remained intense, in hotbeds of religion or politics, there was no place for these phenomena; as soon as various factors intervened and created a sort of social hesitancy, they appeared.

We may, then, attempt a broad classification of the collaborators. They were recruited from the marginal elements of the major political parties, examples being Déat and Marquet,[6] who were not able to settle in the Socialist Party (La Section Française de l'Internationale Ouvrière), and Doriot,[7] who was expelled from the Communist Party. And from among the intellectuals who loathed the bourgeoisie, their class of origin, but did not have the courage, or simply the opportunity, to join the proletariat—examples here

---

6 Adrien Marquet (1885–1955): one-time socialist mayor of Bordeaux; was Minister of the Interior under the Vichy regime for a brief period in 1940.

7 Jacques Doriot (1898–1945): former leading Communist and founder of the Parti Populaire Français, one of France's larger authentically fascist movements.

being Drieu la Rochelle,[8] who had a lifelong obsession with both Italian Fascism and Russian Communism, and Ramon Fernandez[9] who was close to communism for a while but abandoned the Communist Party for the PPF because, as he put it, 'I prefer trains that are departing' (this perpetual oscillation between fascism and communism is typical of the disintegrative forces at work in the marginal zones of the bourgeoisie). Failures in journalism, the arts or the teaching profession make up another category, as in the case of Alain Laubreaux,[10] who was a critic on *Je Suis Partout.*[11] Having arrived from Nouméa (New Caledonia) hoping to take Paris by storm, he never gained acceptance and, after being floored on his arrival in France by a trial for plagiarism, he wavered for a long time between Right and Left, was a disloyal secretary to Henri Béraud[12] and subsequently a staff writer on *La*

8 Pierre Drieu la Rochelle (1893–1945): prominent fascist novelist and essayist.

9 Ramon Fernandez (1894–1944): fascist novelist and literary critic.

10 Alain Laubreaux (1899–1968): French fascist journalist.

11 A weekly newspaper, founded in 1930 under the editorship of the historian Pierre Gaxotte, notorious after 1932 for its pro-fascist leanings.

12 Henri Béraud (1888–1958): leading French journalist who began with Leftist affiliations (he wrote, most notably, for *Le Canard enchainé*) but later drifted towards the far Right. He

Dépêche de Toulouse, the great Radical–Socialist news-paper of the South-West, before ending up in the ranks of the French neo-fascists.

But in a community there are not just individual cases of disintegration: whole groups may be wrenched from the collectivity by forces exerted on them from outside. For example, it is ultramontanism that explains the collaborationist attitude of certain members of the higher clergy. Even before they came into contact with the occupying powers, they felt a kind of attraction towards Rome that acted as an unbalancing force. By contrast, the lower clergy, solidly rooted in French soil and of a Gallican persuasion far removed from Rome, turned out as a whole to be fierce resisters. Most importantly, for want of the will or capacity fully to implement its principles, the French Revolution left in existence on the fringes of the democratic community an outcast element that has survived into our own day. It would be an exaggeration to argue, as some have, that France has been cut in two since 1789. But, in fact, while the majority of bourgeois came to terms with a capitalist democracy that enshrined the free-enterprise regime, a small section of the bourgeois class remained outside French national life because it

---

was condemned to death in 1944 for 'intelligence with the enemy' but was pardoned by de Gaulle.

refused to adapt to the republican constitution. For the 'internal exiles', the royalists of Action française[13] or the fascists of *Je Suis Partout*, France's collapse in 1940 meant first and foremost the end of the Republic. Having no real ties with contemporary France, with our great political traditions, with a century and a half of our history and culture, there was nothing to protect them from the force of attraction exerted by a foreign community.

It is in this way that we can explain this curious paradox: the majority of collaborators were recruited from among what have been dubbed 'Right-wing anarchists'. They accepted none of the Republic's laws, declared themselves free to reject taxation or war, resorted to violence against their opponents despite the rights recognized by our constitution. And yet they based their indiscipline and violence on a conception of a rigorous order; and when they offered their services to a foreign power, it was quite naturally the case that that power was subject to a dictatorial regime. The fact is that these elements, whose anarchy was merely a mark of their profound disintegration, had always wished, in compensation, for a radical integration, precisely because their disintegration was

---

13 Founded in 1898, the Action française was France's leading monarchist organization. Its chief ideologues were Charles Maurras and Léon Daudet (son of the more famous Alphonse de Châteaubriant).

something *suffered*, not desired. They have never taken responsibility for their anarchic freedom, never taken ownership of it; they did not have the courage to draw the logical consequences from their rigorously individualist attitudes. Rather, they kept up, on the margins of actual society, the dream of an authoritarian society into which they could merge and integrate themselves. So they preferred the order the German state seemed to represent for them to the national reality from which they were excluded.

So no class, as such, bears the responsibility for collaboration. And collaboration is not even indicative, as has been argued, of a weakening of the democratic ideal: it merely shows up the effects, within contem- porary communities, of the normal play of the social forces of disintegration. The socially outcast element, which is practically negligible in peacetime, becomes very important in cases of defeat followed by occupation. It would be unjust to call the bourgeoisie a collaborator 'class'. But we can, and must, judge it as a class by the fact that the collaborators were recruited almost exclusively from within it. This is sufficient to show that it has lost its ideology, its force and its internal cohesion.

It is not enough just to have determined the social space of collaboration: there is a psychology of the collaborator from which we can draw some precious lessons. We may, of course, decide from the outset that treason   is always motivated by self-interest and ambition. But, though that broad-brush psychology perhaps makes classification and condemnation easier, it does not entirely correspond to reality. There were disinterested collaborators who silently wished for a German victory without deriving any advantage from their sympathies. Most of those who wrote for the press or took positions in government were, admittedly, ambitious and unscrupulous, but there were also some who occupied positions before the war that were important enough to spare them the need for treason.

And what a strange ambition: if this passion is, ultimately, the pursuit of absolute power over human beings, there was a glaring contradiction in the ambition of the collaborator who, even if he had been made leader of the French pseudo-government, could only ever have been an agent of transmission. It was not his personal prestige but the force of the occupying armies that gave him his authority. Maintained in place by foreign armies, he could only be the agent of an alien power. Though apparently first among the French, he would, if Nazism had triumphed, have been only the thousandth most important man in Europe. Real ambition, if moral principles had not sufficed, ought to have led him to join the Resistance: the leader of a little band of *maquisards* had more scope for action, more prestige and real authority than Laval ever had. If we want to understand the attitude of the collaborators we must, then, examine them dispassionately and describe them objectively on the basis of their words and deeds.

Self-evidently, they all believed, primarily, in a German victory. One cannot imagine a journalist, writer, industrialist or politician who would have chosen to profit from the advantages of Occupation only for four years, knowing or sensing that his escapade would end in imprisonment or death. But this intellectual error, which enables us to understand their attitude, cannot be a justification for it. I knew lots of people in 1940 who thought Britain was finished; the weak gave in to despair, others walled themselves up in an ivory tower and yet others, out of truth to their principles, commenced resistance, taking the view that Germany had won the war but that it was within their power to make it lose the peace. If the collaborators concluded from the Germany victory that it was necessary to subject themselves to the authority of the Reich, this was because they had already taken a profound, original decision that formed the bedrock of their personality: the decision to bow to the fait accompli, whatever it may be. This initial tendency, which they themselves adorned with the name of 'realism', has deep roots in the ideology of our times.

The collaborator suffers from that intellectual illness that may be called historicism. And history does indeed teach us that a great collective event, as soon as it appears, arouses hatred and resistance, which, though sometimes very fine, will later be regarded as ineffectual. As the collaborators saw it, those who devoted their lives to a lost cause may well be seen as fine figures of men, but they were, nonetheless, behind the times and out of step with reality. Such people die twice, because the principles by which they lived are also buried with them. By contrast, the promoters of the historical event, be they Caesar, Napoleon or Henry Ford, will perhaps meet with opprobrium in their own day from the standpoint of a particular ethics, but fifty or a hundred years later only their effectiveness will be remembered and they will be judged by principles they themselves laid down.

A hundred times, among the most honest professors of history and in the most objective of books, I have found this tendency to ratify events simply because they have occurred. They are here confusing the need, insofar as they are scholars, to submit to the facts, with a certain inclination, insofar as they are moral agents, to approve those facts morally. The collaborators took over this philosophy of history. For them, the dominion of the facts went together with a vague belief in progress, but a decapitated progress.

The classical notion of progress in fact assumes an ascent that carries it continually towards an ideal end point. The collaborators regard themselves as too matter-of-fact to believe, without evidence, in this ideal end-point and, hence to believe in the meaning of history. But, though they reject these metaphysical interpretations in the name of science, they do not, for all that, abandon the idea of progress: it merges, in their view, with the march of history. They do not know where they are going but, since they are changing, they must be getting better. The latest historical phenomenon is the best simply because it is the latest: they dimly perceive that it contributes to shaping the face of humanity, that rough sketch which, with each passing moment, acquires a new inflection; they are seized by a kind of pithiatism, abandon themselves passively to the various emerging currents and float towards an unknown destination; they experience the delights of not thinking, of not looking ahead and of accepting the obscure transformations that necessarily turn us into new and unpredictable human beings.

Realism here conceals the fear of performing the customary work of the human being—that stubborn, narrow work that consists in saying 'yes' or 'no' in accordance with principles, in 'undertaking without hope and persevering without success'—and a mystical appetite for mystery, a docile attitude towards a future one has stopped trying to shape; one confines oneself merely to foretelling. Poorly digested Hegelianism has, of course, its part to play in this too. Violence is accepted because all great changes are based on violence and an obscure moral virtue is ascribed to force. Thus, in the assessment of his actions, the collaborator positions himself in the most distant future. His moving closer to Germany, in opposition to Britain, seemed to us a failure to honour a commitment, an unjustifiable breach of his word. The collaborator, though living in our century, judged it from the standpoint of future centuries, precisely as the historian judges the policies of Frederick II. He had found a name for it; it was, quite simply, a 'reversal of alliances' for which there were numerous precedents in history.

This way of judging events in the light of the future was, I think, one of the temptations of defeat for all French people. It represented a subtle form of escapism. By jumping forward a few centuries and, from thence, looking back on the present to contemplate it from afar and resituate it in history, one helped turn it into something past and disguise its unbearable character. The desire was to forget a crushing defeat by envisaging it only in terms of its historical consequences. But this was to forget that history, though it is understood retrospectively and in great swathes, is something that is lived and made day by day. This choice of the historicist attitude and this continual 'pastifying' of the present are typical of the collaborators.

The least guilty are disillusioned idealists who, weary of proposing their ideals in vain, came suddenly to believe that they had to be imposed. If, for example, so many collaborators came from French pacifist ranks, that is because the pacifists, incapable of staving off war, had suddenly decided to see the German army as the force that would bring about peace. Their method had, until that point, been one of propaganda and education. It had proved ineffective. So they persuaded themselves that they were merely changing their methods: they transported themselves into the future to judge present events and, from thence, they saw the Nazi victory bringing a *pax germanica* to the world that was comparable with the famous *pax romana*. The conflict with Russia, then with America, did not open their eyes: they saw these simply as necessary evils. Thus was born one of the most curious paradoxes of our times: the alliance between the most ardent pacifists and the soldiers of a warrior society.

By his docile attitude to facts—or, rather to the single fact of French defeat—the 'realist' collaborator produces an inverted morality: instead of judging facts in the light of what is right, he bases what is right upon what *is*. His implicit metaphysics identifies *is* with *ought*. All that *is* is good; what is good is what *is*. On these principles he hastily builds an ethics of manliness. Borrowing from Descartes the maxim, 'Attempt to conquer yourself, rather than the world', he thinks submission to the facts schools him in courage and manly toughness. In his view, whatever does not start out from an objective appreciation of the situation is the mere fantasy of women and daydreamers. He explains the Resistance not in terms of the assertion of values, but as an anachronistic attachment to dead ways and a dead ideology.

Yet he conceals from himself this deep-seated contradiction: that he too has *chosen* the facts on which he bases his position. The military power of Russia, the industrial power of America, the stubborn resistance of Britain under the 'blitz', the revolt of the enslaved Europeans and the aspiration of human beings to dignity and freedom are also facts. But he has chosen, in the name of realism, not to take account of them. Hence the internal weakness of his system: this man who talks constantly of the 'hard lessons of fact' has selected only those facts favourable to his doctrine. He is perpetually dishonest in his haste to set inconvenient facts aside. A fortnight after the German armies entered Russia, for example, Marcel Déat happily wrote: 'Now that the Russian colossus has collapsed . . .'.

Believing German victory to be achieved already, the collaborator aims to replace legal relations of reciprocity and equality between nations by a kind of feudal bond between suzerain and vassal. Alphonse de

Châteaubriant[14] sees himself as Hitler's liege man. Not being integrated into French society and subject to the universal laws of a community, collaborators attempt to integrate themselves into a new system in which relationships obtain solely on a singular, person-to-person basis. Their realism helps them to do this: the cult of the singular fact and the contempt for Right, which is a universal, leads them to submit themselves to rigorously individual realities: a man, a party or a foreign nation.

As a result, the collaborator's morality, which is variable and contradictory, will be pure obedience to the suzerain's whim. Déat contradicts himself a hundred times, depending on the orders that come down to him from Abetz.[15] He is untroubled by this: the coherence of his attitude consists precisely in changing his point of view as often as his master wishes. But this feudal submission is not itself without its deep contradictions.

If Machiavelli is the dictators' guru, Talleyrand is the model for collaborators. The ambitious collaborator contents himself with a subordinate role, but this is because he believes he has a hand he can play.

---

14 Alphonse de Châteaubriant (1877–1951): Goncourt-winning novelist and exuberant pro-Nazi ideologue.

15 Otto Abetz (1903–58): German ambassador to Paris during the Second World War and a close friend of Jean Luchaire (see note 5).

His loyalty to Germany is conditional. During the Occupation, how many Vichy or Paris politicians kept saying: 'The Germans are children. They have an inferiority complex where France is concerned: we'll do with them as we like'? Some envisaged taking over the 'star supporting role' from the Italians; others took the view that their hour would come when Germany and America would want a third power to open negotiations between them.

Having settled on *force* as the source of Right and as the master's prerogative, the collaborators saw *cunning* as theirs. They recognized their weakness, then, and these high priests of manly power and masculine virtues adapted to using the weapons of the weak—women's weapons. Throughout the articles of Châteaubriant, Drieu and Brasillach,[16] one finds curious metaphors that present relations between France and Germany from the angle of a sexual union in which France plays the female role. And the feudal bond between the collaborator and his master very definitely has a sexual aspect to it.

Insofar as one can imagine the collaborators' state of mind, one senses something like a climate of femininity. The collaborator speaks in terms of force, but he does not possess force. He has the cunning and

16 Robert Brasillach (1909–45): prominent pro-fascist novelist and essayist.

shrewdness that leans on force; he even has charm and seductiveness, since he claims to play on the attraction French culture exerts, in his view, on the Germans. It seems to me there is a strange mixture of masochism and homosexuality here. And Parisian homosexual circles provided many a brilliant recruit.

However, what perhaps amounts to the best psychological explanation of collaboration is hatred. The collaborator seems to dream of a strict feudal order: as we have said, this is the great dream of assimilation for an element of the community that has split away. But it is merely a pipe dream. He actually hates this society, in which he has not been able to play a role. If he dreams of submitting it to the fascist yoke, he does so to enslave it and reduce it practically to the state of a machine. It is typical that Déat, Luchaire and Darnand[17] were perfectly aware of their unpopularity. A hundred times they wrote with absolute lucidity that the immense majority of the country disapproved of their policies. But they had no thought of deploring the indignation and fury they aroused: they needed them. Through that indignation and fury, they brought into being, as an impotent and vainly rebellious totality beneath them, that French community into which they had been unable to merge—

17 Joseph Darnand (1897–1945): head of the notorious Vichy *Milice*. Executed for collaboration.

which excluded them. Since they could not succeed within that community from the inside, they would bring it to heel from the outside; to violate that proud nation, they would integrate themselves into German Europe. Being Hitler's slaves mattered little to them if they could infect the whole of France with that slavery. This was the particular nature of their ambition.

With Drieu la Rochelle, things were not so simple: he started out by hating himself. For twenty years he depicted himself as unhinged, a split personality, a waste of space, dreaming of an iron discipline for himself that he could not spontaneously provide. But, as his novel *Gilles* attests, this self-hatred became a hatred of humanity. Unable to bear the harsh truth that he was 'a weak, spineless child', incapable of mastering his passions, he tried to see himself as a typical product of an entirely rotten society. He dreamt of fascism for that society, whereas all that was needed was to lay down some strict rules of conduct for himself. He wanted to eliminate the human element from himself and others by transforming human societies into anthills. For this pessimist, the coming of fascism corresponded, ultimately, to the suicide of humanity.

Realism, rejection of the universal, anarchy and the dream of an iron discipline, the defence of violence and cunning, femininity, hatred of humanity—so many characteristics that can be explained by disintegration. The collaborator, whether or not he has the opportunity to manifest himself as such, is an enemy democratic societies perpetually carry within them. If we want to avoid that enemy surviving the war in other forms, it is not enough just to execute a few traitors. We must, as far as possible, complete the unification of French society or, in other words, the task begun by the 1789 Revolution. And this can be achieved only by a new revolution, the one that was attempted in 1830, 1848 and 1871 and which was always followed by counter-revolution. Democracy has always been a nursery for fascists because, by its nature, it tolerates all opinions. We should, at last, pass some restrictive laws: there must be no freedom to oppose freedom.

And since the collaborator's favourite argument— and the fascist's—is *realism*, we should take advantage of our victory to confirm the failure of all realist politics. One ought, of course, to come to terms with the facts, to draw lessons from experience. But this flexibility, this political positivism must be only a means for achieving an end that is not subordinate to the facts and that does not derive its existence from them. By providing the example of a politics based on principles, we shall be contributing to ridding the world of the species of 'pseudo-realists'. By contrast, the Resistance, which won out in the end, has shown that the role of human beings is to know how to say 'no' to the facts, even when it seems one must bow down before them. Admittedly, one has to try to conquer oneself rather than vanquish fortune but if one has to conquer oneself first, one does so, ultimately, the better to vanquish fortune.

La République française (New York, August 1945)

*

THE END OF THE WAR

People had been told to put out flags. They did not. The war ended in indifference and anxiety.

Nothing had changed in everyday life. The booming of the radio, the bold type of the newspapers were not able to persuade us. We would have liked some sort of marvel, a sign in the heavens, to prove to us that peace had written itself into things. A puny gun coughed on a boring summer's afternoon. People went by on the bridges and in the streets with lifeless eyes, busy with their chronic hunger and their own concerns.

How are we, with our empty stomachs, to rejoice at the end of this war that just goes on ending and which, after ravaging our land, has gone off to die at the back of beyond, around those islands whose name reminds us of double almonds and family betting games.[1] And what an abstract end. There may, it seems, be turmoil in Japan; the Japanese army is counter-attacking in Manchuria and the emperor and his captains speak of impending revenge; the Chinese are on the verge of civil war. And, in the background, immense emergent powers eye each other with some surprise and a formal coldness, weighing each other up and keeping a respectful distance, like those wrestlers who rapidly stroke each other's forearms and shoulders before coming to grips.

Yet certain men in their offices have decided the war is over. One of them announces it, speaking at a microphone, a piece of paper in his hand. To believe him, we would have had not to have learned to disbelieve the words of men who come to microphones with pieces of paper in their hands. It is not that one dares imagine he is lying. One merely thinks this whole business of war and peace unfolds at a certain level of truth: the truth of historical declarations, military parades and commemorative ceremonies. People look at each other with a vague sense of disappointment: is this all that Peace is?

It isn't Peace. Peace is a beginning. We are living through death throes. For a long time we thought War

---

1 By a French tradition of obscure origin, when someone finds a double almond and shares it, the first of the two to shout 'Philippine' after midnight wins a gift from the other.

and Peace were two clearly distinct entities, like Black and White or Hot and Cold. It wasn't true and today we know it. Between 1934 and 1939, we learned that Peace can end without war breaking out. We are familiar with the exquisite subtleties of armed neutrality, intervention and pre-belligerency. The movement from peace to war in our century is a matter of continuous gradations. On the most optimistic view, we are going to have to go through this process in the opposite direction. Today, 20 August 1945, in this deserted, starving Paris, the War has ended but Peace has not begun.

Peace seemed to us like a *return*. A return of the roaring twenties, a return of French prosperity and greatness. In wartime, people always look forward to the peace of their youth: they confuse youth and peace. It is always a different peace that comes. The one that is vaguely in the air now, beyond the final storms, is an enormous world peace, in which France has only a very small place.

The little gun that was coughing the other afternoon confirmed France's slide—and that of Europe. A verdict delivered at the other end of the earth told us that the time of our shame and pain was at an end. All that remained was to say 'thank you'. That meant we had to rebuild France, taking account of its new limitations. The veil of illusion that had masked its real level of importance for fifty years had been torn at the very moment of Japanese capitulation. We men of forty have been saying for some time that France has, above all, to resign itself to playing a minor role. But we are so used to seeing it in major ones that we speak of it not as an ageing actress, but as a star who, for some moral reason, would have to agree for a time to pass incognito. However, a more austere younger generation is coming up behind us, a generation better suited to the new tasks, because it has known only a humiliated France. These young people are the men of the Peace. We were the men of a lost battle, of a war that is fizzling out. Will we be stragglers in the coming years; will we be lost souls? This war's end is also a little bit our own or, at least, it is the end of our youth.

We believed, on no evidential basis, that peace was the natural state and substance of the universe, that war was merely a temporary agitation of its surface. Today we recognize our error: the end of the war is quite simply the end of *this* war. The future has not yet begun: we no longer believe in the end of wars; and we are so used to the sound of arms, so benumbed by our injuries and hunger, that we no longer even quite manage wholly to wish for it. If someone told us tomorrow that a new conflict had broken out, we would say, with a resigned shrug, 'That's only to be expected.' Moreover, among the best of men, I find a silent consent to war, something like a commitment to the full tragedy of the human condition.

Pacifism still had in it the hope that one day, by patience and purity, we would bring about heaven on earth. The pacifists still believed it was humanity's birthright that things should not always go badly. Today, I see a lot of modest, thoughtful young people who lay claim to no rights, not even the right to hope. They loathe violence, but are not optimistic enough— are too practical—to dare to think we shall be able to do without it. I saw some who refused to report their precarious state of health to the recruiting board for fear of being declared unfit for service. 'I would look an idiot,' they would say, 'at the next war.' So it seems that this war, much more atrocious than the last, has left memories that are less bad. Perhaps because we believed for a long time that it was less stupid. It did not seem stupid to fight German imperialism, to resist the army of occupation.

It is only today that we see Mussolini, Hitler and Hiro Hito were merely petty tyrants. These rapacious, sanguinary powers that fell upon the democracies were, by a long way, the weakest nations. The petty tyrants are dead and fallen, their little feudal princi-palities of Germany, Italy and Japan are brought low. The world is simplified. Two giants stand alone and are not well disposed to one another. But it will be some time before this war reveals its true face. Its last moments served to remind us of human frailty. So, we are happy that it is ending, but not with the way it is ending.

A good number of Europeans would have preferred Japan to be invaded, crushed by naval bombardment. But the little bomb that can kill a hundred thousand at a stroke and which, tomorrow, will kill 2 million, brings us up suddenly against our responsibilities. The next time, the earth could be blown up: that absurd end would leave forever in suspense the problems that have been our concern for over ten thousand years. No one would ever know whether humanity could have overcome racial hatred, whether it would have found a solution to class struggles. When one thinks of it, everything seems futile. And yet humanity had, one day, to come into possession of its death. Up until now it had led a life that came to it from who knows where and—since it lacked the means to commit suicide—it didn't even have the power to reject self-inflicted death.

Wars made little crater-shaped holes, quickly filled in, among this compact mass of the living. Everyone was safe in the crowd, protected from the antediluvian nothingness by the generations of their ancestors, from the future nothingness by the generations of their descendants—always in the middle of time, never at the extremes. And yet, here we are, back at the millennium. Each morning, we shall be on the eve of the end of time, on the eve of the day when our honesty, courage and goodwill will no longer have any meaning for anyone, and will perish, together with ill-will, spite and fear, no distinction remaining between them. After the death of God, the death of man is now announced.

From this point on, my freedom is purer: this act I commit today will have neither God nor man as its everlasting witness. I have to be, now and for all eternity, my own witness. I have to be moral on this booby-trapped earth because I want to be. And if the whole of humanity continues to live, it will do so not simply because it has been born but because it will have decided to prolong its life. There is no longer any *human species*. The community that has appointed itself guardian of the atom bomb stands above the realm of nature, being responsible now for its life and death. It will be necessary every day, every minute, for it to consent to live. This is what we are anxiously feeling today. 'But no,' you will say, 'we are quite simply at the mercy of a madman.' That is not true: the atom bomb isn't available to any old lunatic; that madman would have to be a Hitler and, as with the original Führer, we would all be responsible for the emergence of a new one. So, just as this war is coming to an end, we have come full circle. In each of us humanity discovers its potential death, takes responsibility for its life and death.

Should we give up the idea of building this peace, the most perilous of all, because we no longer believe in Peace, because our country has lost many of its powers, because the potential suicide of the earth taints our undertakings with a subtle nothingness? Quite the contrary. I can understand, but cannot condone, the sentiments of that young Russian woman, a naturalized French citizen since childhood, who wept on the day of victory, saying, 'I'm from a little country! I'm from a little country and I want to be from a big country that's genuinely victorious.' And yet she was Russian by birth: perhaps she was nostalgic for her country of origin. But what do we who were born in France have to say? To say this is our homeland is not much. Most importantly, it is vague.

France is our concrete situation, our opportunity and our lot in life. It is still—more than ever—within national frameworks that personal development takes place. Internationalism, which was a fine dream, is now just the stubborn illusion of a few Trotskyites. What can we do, then? To deny the French community is to deny ourselves. And if we gamble on life, on our friends, on our person, we gamble on France, we commit ourselves to seeking to integrate it into this rough, tough world, into this mortally endangered humanity. We have also to gamble on the earth, even if one day it should be smashed to pieces. Simply because that is where we are.

God is dead. The 'sacred, inalienable rights' are dead and buried. The war is dead and with it have gone the justifications and alibis it offered to weak souls, the hopes of a gentle and just peace it kept alive in people's hearts. 'Up to now I lived in anxiety,' said Tristan Bernard when they came to arrest him. 'Now I shall live in hope.' On the day of Japanese surrender, we would be able to say precisely the opposite. No longer shall we read each morning in the newspapers the comforting news of a minor or major German defeat. The dailies will tell us of the rebirth of the military spirit in Germany, of civil war in China, of the diplomatic difficulties encountered by the Three, the Four or the Five. But we have to gamble. As it dies, the war leaves man naked and without illusions; he is abandoned now to its own devices, having at last understood that he has only himself to rely on. This is the only good piece of news that thin, ceremonious burst of gunfire brought us the other afternoon.

Les Temps modernes (October 1945)

*

INDIVIDUALISM AND CONFORMISM
IN THE UNITED STATES

How can you talk about a hundred and thirty-five million Americans? We would need to have lived in this country for ten years and we shall be spending only six weeks here. We are put down in cities where we pick up a few details—yesterday Baltimore, today Knoxville, the day after tomorrow New Orleans—and then, after admiring the biggest factory or the biggest bridge or the biggest dam in the world, we fly off again, our heads full of facts and figures.

We shall have seen more steel and aluminium than human beings. But can one speak about steel? As for 'impressions', they come as and when they please.

Some say, 'Keep to the facts!'

But what facts? The length of this shipyard in feet or the electric blue of the oxyhydrogen torch in the pale light of this shed? In choosing, I am already deciding what America is.

Others, by contrast, say, 'Step back and get some perspective on things!' But I distrust those perspectives that are already generalizations. So I've decided to convey my personal impressions and constructions, taking the responsibility on myself. Perhaps I've dreamed this America. I shall, at any rate, be honest with my dream: I shall set it out just as I dreamed it.

And today I would like to give you my impression of those two contradictory 'slogans' doing the rounds in Paris: 'the American is a conformist' and 'the American is an individualist'.

Like everyone else, I had heard tell of the famous American 'melting pot' which, at various critical temperatures, transforms a Pole, an Italian and a Finn into citizens of the United States. But I did not quite know what it meant.

Well, on the very day after I arrived I met a European in the process of 'melting'. In the main lobby of the Plaza Hotel I was introduced to a dark-haired man of quite modest stature who, like everyone here, talked with a slightly nasal twang, without visible movement of his lips or cheeks, who laughed with his mouth, but not with his eyes, and who expressed himself in a good, but heavily accented French, his speech sprinkled with barbarisms and Americanisms.

When I complimented him on his knowledge of our language, he replied with astonishment, 'But that's because I'm French.' He was born in Paris, has been living in American for only fifteen years and, before the war, went back to France every six months. Yet he is already half in the grip of America. His mother has never left Paris: when he speaks of *Paname* in deliberately vulgar tones he sounds much more like a Yankee wanting to show off his knowledge of Europe than an exiled Frenchman recalling his homeland. He feels obliged from time to time to cast roguish winks in my direction, saying 'Aha! New Orleans, fine women!' But, in so doing, he is conforming more to the American's idea of the Frenchman than seeking collusion with a compatriot. 'Fine women', and he laughs, but in a forced way. Puritanism isn't far off and I feel a chill run down my spine.

I felt as though I were present at an Ovidian metamorphosis: the man's face was still too expressive, it retained that faintly annoying mimicry of intelligence by which you can recognize a French face anywhere. But he would soon be a tree or a rock. I wondered with some curiosity what powerful forces had to be brought into play to achieve such integrations and disintegrations so surely and swiftly.

Now, these forces are mild and persuasive. You have only to walk the streets, enter a shop or switch on a radio to encounter them, to feel their effect on you like a warm breath.

In America—at least the America I know—you are never alone in the street. The walls speak to you. To left and right of you there are posters, illuminated advertisements and enormous shop windows simply containing large boards with photomontages or tables of statistics. Here, you have a distraught woman leaning over to kiss an American soldier, there, a plane dropping bombs on a village, and, beneath the picture, the words, 'Bibles, not bombs'. The nation walks with you. It proffers advice and commands. But it does so sotto voce and is careful to explain its orders in minute detail. There is no injunction that is not accompanied by a brief commentary or a justificatory image, whether in an advert for cosmetics (Today, more than ever, you have to be beautiful. Take care of your face for when *he* comes home: buy cream X.) or in propaganda for War Bonds.

I dined yesterday in a restaurant at Fontana, an artificial village built around a great dam in Tennessee.

All along the road leading to that dam, a road full of lorries, automobiles and pick-up trucks, a great hoarding conveys a parable in cartoon form on the subject of working together. Two donkeys roped together are trying to reach two piles of hay some distance apart. Each pulls on the rope in its own direction and they are half-strangling each other. Finally, they understand. They move together and begin merrily munching the first pile together. When they have eaten it, we see them starting out in unison towards the second.

Clearly, it was a deliberate decision to banish all commentary. The passers-by *have to* draw the conclusion *themselves*. No violence is done to them. On the contrary, the image is an appeal to their intelligence. They are obliged to interpret and understand it. It does not bludgeon them, as Nazi propaganda did with its garish posters. It remains low-key. It requires participation if it is to be deciphered. When they have understood, it is as though they had formed the idea themselves. They are already more than half convinced.

In the factories, they have put up loudspeakers everywhere. These are intended to combat the workers' isolation in their encounter with matter.

Walking through the immense naval dockyard near Baltimore, you first encounter that human dispersal, that great solitude of the workers so familiar to us in Europe. Masked men, bending over steel plates, spend all day working with their oxyhydrogen torches. But as soon as they put on their headphones, they can hear music. And the music is already guidance insinuating itself stealthily into them, it is already a guided dream. And then the music stops and they receive information about the war or their work.

When we left Fontana, the engineer who had so kindly taken us everywhere led us into a little glass room where a new wax disc was revolving, readied for the recording of our voices. He explained that all the visitors who had visited the dam had summed up their impressions at the microphone before they left. We were not about to refuse such a kind host. Those of us who knew English spoke and our words were recorded. The next day they would be broadcast in the dockyard, in the canteen and to all the houses in the village, and the workers would be encouraged to continue their good work, learning with pleasure of the excellent impression they had made on a group of foreigners.

Add to this the advice meted out by the radio and in the columns of the newspapers and, particularly, the activities of the countless voluntary organizations whose aims are almost always educational, and you will see that the American citizen is tightly hedged about.

But it would be an error to see this as an oppressive manoeuvre on the part of the government or big American capitalists.

The present government is, of course, at war. It is obliged, for purposes of war propaganda, to use such methods. Doubtless, too, one of its main concerns is education.

In Tennessee, for example, where the farmers ruined the soil by the repeated planting of maize, it is trying to teach them gradually to allow the soil to rest by varying their crops each year. To achieve its goal, it has combined gifts (low-cost electricity, free irrigation) with argument. But what we have here is a much more spontaneous and diffuse phenomenon.

This educative tendency really springs from the heart of the community. Every American is educated by other Americans and educates others in turn. All over New York, both in the schools and outside, there are courses in Americanization.

And they teach everything: sewing, cooking, even romance. There is a course in a New York school on how a girl should go about getting her boyfriend to marry her. In all this, it is not so much a question of training a human being as training a pure American. But Americans make no distinction between American reason and reason *tout court*. All the advice with which their route is studded is so perfectly motivated, so penetrating, that they feel themselves cradled by an immense solicitude that never leaves them helpless or alone.

I have met some of these 'modern' mothers who have never ordered their children to do anything without first persuading them to obey. They have acquired a more total, and perhaps more formidable, authority over them than if they had used threats and blows. In the same way, the American, whose reason and freedom are appealed to at every hour of the day, makes it a point of honour to do what he is asked. It is by acting like everyone else that he feels both most reasonable and most American; it is by displaying the greatest conformism that he feels most free.

So far as I can judge, the characteristics of the American nation are the opposite of those which Hitler gave to Germany and Maurras wanted to give to France.

For Hitler (or Maurras), an argument is good for Germany if, first of all, it is German. It is always suspect if it has any slight whiff of universality.

By contrast, it is the peculiar characteristic of the American that he regards his thought as universal. One can detect a Puritan influence here which I need not go into at this point. But there is, above all, this concrete, daily presence of a flesh-and-blood Reason, a Reason you can see. Most of the people I spoke to seemed to have a naive, passionate faith in the virtues of Reason. One evening an American said to me, 'If international politics were carried on by reasonable, sane men, wouldn't war be abolished forever?' Some French people present pointed out that the matter was not so straightforward and he grew angry. 'All right,' he said, with indignant contempt, 'go and build graveyards!' I, for my part, said nothing. Discussion between us was not possible. I believe in evil and he does not.

It is this Rousseauesque optimism which distances the American from our standpoint where Nazi Germany is concerned. In order to accept the atrocities, he would have to accept that man can be wholly evil. 'Do you believe there are two Germanies?' an American doctor asked me. I replied that I did not.

'I understand,' he said. 'You can't think otherwise because France has suffered so much. But it's a pity.'

Machines play a part here. They too are universalizing factors. With mechanical objects, there is generally only one way to use them; the one indicated in the accompanying leaflet. The American uses his mechanical corkscrew, his fridge or his automobile at the same time as all the other Americans and in the same way. Besides, the object is not made to order. It is for anyone and   will work for anyone, provided he knows how to use it properly.

So, when the American puts his nickel in the slot in the tram, the subway or the drinks machine, he feels like anyone. Not like an anonymous unit, but like a person who has divested himself of his individuality and elevated himself to the impersonality of the Universal.

It was this total freedom in conformism that struck me first. No city is freer than New York. You can do as you like there. Public opinion itself keeps order. The few Americans I met seemed conformist out of freedom, depersonalized by rationalism, and they identified universal Reason with their own particular Nation as part of a single creed.

But almost immediately I discovered their profound individualism. This combination of social conformism and individualism is perhaps what a Frenchman will have the greatest difficulty understanding. For us, individualism has retained the old, classical form of 'the individual's struggle against society and, particularly, against the state'. This is not what it means in America. First, the state was for a long time only an administrative body. For some years now, it has tended to play a different role, but this has not changed the Americans' feelings towards it. It is 'their' state, it is the expression of 'their' nation: they have a deep respect and a proprietary love for it.[1]

---

1 When a gang of Rassemblement du peuple français supporters attempted to disrupt a political meeting in which I was taking part, a brawl ensued. An American who shared our ideas was amazed we did not call the police. I explained our reluctance, but he was still rather disconcerted: 'In our country,' he said, 'the police belong to all the citizens. We find it *natural* to call them in.'

If you just walk about in New York for a few days, you cannot help but notice the profound link between American conformism and individuality. Taken lengthwise and from side to side, New York, laid flat, is the most conformist city in the world. If you except old Broadway, then from Washington Square not one street curves or runs diagonally. Some ten long parallel furrows run straight from the tip of Manhattan to the Harlem River. These are the avenues and they are crossed by hundreds of smaller furrows that are strictly perpendicular to them.

This grid pattern is New York: the streets are so alike that they have not been given names; like soldiers, they have merely been assigned a number.

But look up and everything changes. Viewed in terms of height, New York is the triumph of individualism. The buildings escape upwards from planning regulations. They have twenty-five, fifty-five or a hundred storeys; they are grey, brown, white, Moorish, medieval, renaissance or modern. On Lower Broadway they press up against each other, dwarfing tiny black churches, and then suddenly they spread out, leaving a gaping hole of light between them. Seen from Brooklyn, they seemed to me to have the solitude and nobility of the clumps of palm trees by the rivers in the Moroccan Souss: clumps of skyscrapers which the eye is always trying to bind together and which always come apart.

So American individualism seemed to me, initially, like a third dimension. In no sense is it opposed to conformism. Indeed, it presupposes it. But within conformism it is a new direction, upwards and downwards.

First there is the struggle for existence—and it is very harsh. Every individual wants to succeed—that is to say, to make money. But we should not see this as greed, nor even as a taste for luxury. It seems to me that in the USA, money is merely the necessary, but symbolic, token of success. You must succeed, because success proves your moral virtue and intelligence, and because it indicates that you enjoy divine protection.

And you must succeed because only then can you stand out from the crowd as a person. Take the American newspapers. Until you are a success, there is no point hoping that your articles will be published in the form in which you submitted them. They will be cut and pruned. But if you have a name that makes money, all that changes. What you write will go through without editing. You have acquired the right to be yourself.

It is the same in the theatre. A lady very well-versed in French literature and well-known in publishing circles asked me if I would like to have a play put on in the States. I replied that I would be happy to, if the directors were not, as I had been told, in the habit of reworking the scripts submitted to them. She seemed most surprised and said, 'If they don't do it, who will? What you wrote is meant to be read. But they have to work on it, so that it can be understood.'[2]

So, individualism in America is, above all, each person's passionate aspiration, in the struggle for existence, to the state of individual. There are individuals in America the way there are skyscrapers. There's Ford, there's Rockefeller, there's Hemingway, there's Roosevelt: they are models and examples.

In this sense, the office blocks are votive offerings to success. Behind the Statue of Liberty, they are like the statues of a man or an enterprise that have risen above the others. They are huge publicity ventures, built by individuals or groups to demonstrate their financial triumph. Their owners occupy only a small part of the premises and let out the rest. I was not mistaken, then, in taking them to symbolize New York individualism. They quite simply mark the fact that in the United States individuality is something to be achieved. It is no doubt for this reason that New Yorkers seemed to me so passionately attached to a free-market economy.

---

2 Hence the misunderstanding in the Kravchenko case. Since rewriting is accepted practice, Kravchenko is regarded by Americans as the author of his book. We, by contrast, find it hard to see him as such.

Yet everyone knows the power of the trusts in the USA, which represents, all in all, another form of command economy. But the New Yorker hasn't forgotten the day when a man could earn a fortune off his own bat. What he finds distasteful in the command economy is bureaucracy. So, rather paradoxically, this man who allows himself to be led so obediently by the nose in his public and private life is intransigent when it comes to his job. This he regards as the sphere of his independence, initiative and personal dignity.

For everything else, there are the 'associations'. In 1930, there were more than a hundred and fifty headquarters of associations and groups in Washington. I shall mention just one of them, the Foreign Policy Association.

On some seventeenth floor, 'over a cup of tea', we met some of those tall, grey-haired women, who have made up a majority in these associations since the war began; they are amiable but rather cold, and as intelligent as men. They told us how in 1917 a number of people, firmly convinced that the United States was entering the war without knowing anything of foreign affairs, had decided to devote their free time to providing the country with the information it lacked.

The organization has twenty-six thousand members today, with three hundred branches in the various states. It provides documentation to more than five hundred newspapers. Politicians consult its publications. It has, indeed, given up on informing the general public: it now informs the informers (scholars, teachers, priests and journalists). Every week it publishes a bulletin with a study of an international question and commentary on events in Washington and once a fortnight it sends documentation to the newspapers which they reprint in whole or in part.

Can one imagine in the France of 1939 an association of this kind providing Bonnet or Daladier with information and sending its bulletins to Maurras for inclusion in *Action française* and to Cachin for *L'Humanité*?

What struck me most forcefully were our hostess' last words: 'The point,' she said, 'is that we protect the individual. Outside of the associations a man is alone; in the associations he is a person; and he protects himself against each of them by belonging to several.' You can see the meaning of this individualism: the citizen must first fit into a structure and protect himself; he must enter into a social contract with other citizens of his own kind. And it is this smaller community that will confer upon him his individual function and personal worth. Within the association he will take initiatives, will be able to advocate a personal policy and, if he is able to, influence the collective orientation.

Just as the solitary individual arouses distrust in the USA, so this directed, hedged-in individualism is encouraged. This is illustrated, at quite another level, by the attempts made by leaders of industry to foster self-criticism among their staff.

When the worker is in a trade union, when government and managerial propaganda have sufficiently integrated him into the community, *then* he is asked to distinguish himself from the others and show initiative. On more than one occasion, at a factory entrance, we came across brightly coloured booths where improvements proposed by members of the workforce were displayed under glass, together with photographs of their inventors who frequently receive bonuses for their efforts.

I have said enough, I hope, to convey how the American citizen is subjected, from cradle to grave, to an intense force of organization and Americanization; how he is first depersonalized by a constant appeal to his reason, public-spiritedness and freedom; and how, when he is duly slotted into the nation by professional organizations and by the associations for moral edification and education, he suddenly recovers awareness of himself and his personal autonomy. He is then free to escape towards an almost Nietzschean individualism symbolized by the skyscrapers in the clear skies of New York. In any event, it is not individualism that is the basic element here, but conformism. Personality must be won: it is a social function or the affirmation of success.

Le Figaro (March 1945)

＊

CITIES OF AMERICA

The first few days I was lost. I had not adjusted to the skyscrapers, yet they did not amaze me. They did not seem like human constructions inhabited by men but, rather, like those dead parts of the cityscape, those rocks and hills that you find in cities built on rugged terrain and skirt around without even noticing. At the same time I was perpetually looking for something to hold my attention for a moment. Something I never found. A detail, a square perhaps, or a monument. I didn't yet know you have to look at the houses and streets here in bulk.

To learn to live in these cities and to love them as the Americans do, I had to fly over the vast deserts of the west and the south. In Europe, our towns are contiguous. They are immersed in a human countryside that has been worked over yard by yard. And then we are vaguely aware that there is, very far away across the sea, a mythical entity known as the desert. For the American, that myth is a daily reality. Between New Orleans and San Francisco we flew for hours over dry, red earth, studded with grey-green bushes. Suddenly a city welled up, a little grid on the ground, and then once again there was red earth, the savannah, the twisted rocks of the Grand Canyon and the snows of the Rockies.

After a few days of this, I came to see that an American city was, originally, a camp in the desert. People from some far-off place, drawn to the site by a mine, an oilfield or good agricultural land, arrived one fine day and settled there as quickly as they could in a clearing on the banks of a river. They built the essential organs, bank, city hall and church, then wooden bungalows by the hundreds. The road, if there was one, served as a spine; perpendicular to it, they traced out streets like vertebrae. The American towns that have this kind of centre parting are almost too numerous to count.

Nothing has changed since the days of the wagon trains. Each year towns are founded in the United States and they are founded by the same procedures.

Take Fontana in Tennessee, near one of the great TVA[1] dams. Twelve years ago, pine trees grew on the

---

1 Tennessee Valley Authority, created in 1933, by President Franklin D. Roosevelt as part of the New Deal.

red soil of the mountain. As soon as they began to build the dam, they cut down the pine trees and three villages sprang from the soil: two white ones, with three thousand and five thousand inhabitants respectively, and a black one. The workers live there with their families. Four or five years ago, at the height of the works, the birth rate was running at one per day. Half the village has a lakeside air to it. The houses are timber-built with green roofs and have been built on piles to avoid the damp. The other half is made of collapsible dwellings, the so-called prefabricated houses. They too are built of timber; they are constructed some six hundred miles away and loaded onto lorries. When they arrive, it takes just a single team a single day to erect them. The smallest of them cost the employer two thousand dollars and he rents them to his workers at nineteen dollars a month (31 dollars furnished). Inside, with their mass-produced furniture, central heating, electric lights and refrigerators, they are reminiscent of ship's cabins. Every inch of these little antiseptic rooms has been utilized: there are cupboards in the walls and drawers under the bed.

You leave, somewhat weighed down, with the sense of having seen the meticulous, small-scale reconstruction of a 1944 flat in a Year-3000 world. As soon as you set foot outside, you see hundreds of exactly identical dwellings, piled up, squashed against the earth, yet still, in their very shape, retaining a nomadic air of sorts. They look like a caravan scrapyard. The lakeside village and the caravan scrapyard stand facing each other on either side of a road that climbs into the pines. There you have an American town, or rather the matrix of an American town, with all its essential organs. At the bottom a dime store, higher up the clinic, and at the top a 'mixed' church, where they provide what may be termed a basic service, valid for all denominations.

The striking feature is the lightness and fragility of these buildings. The village is weightless. It seems barely to rest on the soil. It has not yet managed to leave a human imprint on this reddish earth and the dark woods. It is *temporary*. And it will, indeed, soon be on the road again. In two years' time, the dam will be finished, the workers will leave and the prefabricated houses will be dismantled and sent to reconstruct another Fontana around an oil-well in Texas or a cotton plantation in Georgia, under different skies and with new residents.

There is nothing exceptional about this roving village. In the USA, towns are born the way they die: in one day. The Americans make no complaint: the main thing for them is to be able to take their homes with them. These 'homes' are the sets of objects, furnishings, photographs and souvenirs that belong to them, that reflect back their image and form the living inner landscape of their dwellings. They are their *Penates* and, like Aeneas, they haul them about everywhere.

The 'house' is the shell: they abandon it on the slightest pretext.

We have workers' settlements in France, but they are sedentary affairs and will never become real cities. They are, rather, the artificial product of neighbouring townships. In America, just as every citizen can in theory become president, so every Fontana can become a Denver or a Minneapolis: it just takes a little luck. Conversely, Denver and Minneapolis are Fontanas that have struck it lucky. To take just one example: in 1905, the population of Detroit was just three hundred thousand. Today, it is 1 million.

The inhabitants are perfectly aware of this luck. In their films and books they like to recall the time when their city was merely an encampment. And that is why they pass so easily from city to encampment: they make no distinction between the two. Detroit and Minneapolis, Knoxville and Memphis were *born temporary* and have remained so. They will doubtless never take to the road again on the back of a lorry. But they remain at melting point; they have never reached an internal solidifying temperature.

What for us would merely be a change of situation is for an American the occasion of a real break with his past. There were many who, when going off to war, sold off their apartments and everything else, even their suits: what point was there in keeping things that would be out of fashion by the time they returned? Soldiers' wives frequently adopt a reduced style of life and move to live more modestly in another part of town. Sadness and faithfulness to the absent soldier are marked by moving house.

Fluctuations in American fortunes are also marked by changes of neighbourhood. It is the rule in the United States for the fashionable areas of town to slide from the centre to the periphery. After five years, the centre is 'decayed'. If you walk around its dirty streets, you will come upon apartment buildings going to rack and ruin, but retaining an air of pretension beneath their filth; you will find complicated architecture—one-storey wooden-framed houses with entrances formed by peristyles supported by columns, Gothic chalets, 'colonial' houses and the like. They were once aristocratic residences; now the poor live there. There are Graeco-Roman temples in Chicago's grim Negro district. They still look good from the outside, but, inside, twelve lice- and rat-infested Negro families are crowded into five or six rooms.

At the same time, changes are continually being made. A block is purchased so that it can be demolished and a bigger block put up on the same site; after five years, it is sold to a developer who tears it down to build a third one. As a result, American cities are moving landscapes, whereas our cities are our protective shells.

Only a very old French person would be able to say what I heard a forty-year-old American say yesterday in Chicago: 'When I was young, this area here was all lake. But they filled in this part of the lake and built on it.' And this morning a thirty-five-year-old lawyer, showing me round the Negro district, said: 'I was born here. It was a white area then. You would not have seen a black person, except for servants. Today the whites have gone and a quarter of a million Negroes are crowded into their houses.'

Mr Verdier, who owns the large 'City of Paris' department store in San Francisco, saw the earthquake and the fire that destroyed three-quarters of the city. He was a young man, then, but he still remembers the disaster perfectly. He watched as the city was rebuilt—in 1913 it still had an Asiatic look to it—and then as it was rapidly Americanized. He has, then, superimposed memories of three San Franciscos.

We Europeans change in changeless cities and our houses and neighbourhoods outlive us. American cities change faster than their residents and it is the residents who outlive the cities.

We are, in fact, visiting the USA in wartime. The frantic liveliness of American cities has suddenly been petrified: there is no more building; hardly anyone moves house. But this stagnation is entirely temporary. The cities have come to a standstill, like a dancer on the screen whose leg stays in the air when the film stops. Everywhere you feel the sap rising that will make them burst into life again as soon as the war ends.

To begin with, there are some urgent problems. For example, the black district of Chicago has to be rebuilt. The government had set about the work before Pearl Harbor, but the buildings it put up can barely house seven thousand, and there are two hundred and fifty thousand to be accommodated. Then the industrialists want to expand and transform their factories: the famous Chicago meatyards are going to be completely modernized.

Lastly, the average American is obsessed with the image of the 'modern house', which is widely advertised and which will, we are told, be a hundred times more comfortable than today's dwellings. The construction of such homes in massive quantities definitely forms part of the 'industrial conversion' projects that are springing up almost everywhere at the moment.

After the war, America will certainly be seized with a real construction fever. The American looks on his city today with objectivity. It does not occur to him to find it ugly, but he finds it decidedly old. If it were even older, as ours are, he could find a social past in it, a tradition. We generally live in our grandfathers' dwellings. Our streets reflect the customs of bygone centuries; they tend to sift out the present a little and nothing of what goes on in the rue Montorgueil or the rue du Pot-de-Fer is entirely of the present. But at thirty years of age, the Americans live in houses that were built when they were twenty.

These houses, too young to look *old*, seem merely outmoded to them. They lag behind their other tools—the cars they can trade in every two years, the refrigerators, the radio sets. That is why they see their cities rationally, without empty sentimentality. They are somewhat attached to them, the way you become attached to a car, but they see them first and foremost as instruments which they will unhesitatingly exchange for handier ones.

For us, a city is, first and foremost, a past. For them, it is mainly a future. What they like in it is everything it has not yet become, everything it can be.

What are the European's impressions when he lands in an American city? First, he thinks he has been 'had'. All the talk has been of skyscrapers, and New York and Chicago have been presented to him as 'cities standing tall'. Now, his first feeling is, on the contrary, that the average height of an American city is very appreciably less than that of a French one. The immense majority of houses are of no more than two storeys. Even in the very big cities, the five-storey block is the exception.

Then he is struck by the lightness of the materials used. In the USA, stone is hardly ever used. The skyscrapers have a metal framework encased in concrete; the other buildings are of brick or timber. Even in the richest cities and the smartest neighbourhoods, one frequently finds timber-built houses. The fine colonial residences of New Orleans are built of wood, as are the pretty chalets where the Hollywood directors live and the 'Californian style' cottages of San Francisco. Everywhere you find groups of timber-built houses crushed between two twenty-storey blocks.

The brick houses are the colour of dried blood or, by contrast, daubed and smeared with green, bright yellow or harsh white.[2] In most of the cities they have no sloping roofs; they are cubes or rectangular parallelepipeds with severely flat facades. All these dwellings, hastily built and deliberately made to be

---

2 Kisling and Masson have often complained that the cityscapes of the United States do not greatly encourage painting. This is partly, I believe, because the cities are already painted. They do not have the hesitant colours of ours. What can one do with these hues that are *already* art—or at least artifice—other than simply leave them where they are?

hastily demolished, are singularly akin, as we have seen, to the 'pre-fabricated houses' of Fontana.

The lightness of these jerry-built constructions, their garish colours alternating with the dark red of the bricks, and the extraordinary variety of decoration on them, though it fails to conceal the uniformity of their pattern, all give a feeling, even in the middle of the city, of walking in the suburbs of a seaside resort. One might be in Trouville, Cabourg or La Baule. Only ephemeral seaside chalets, with their fragility and pretentious architecture, can give an idea of American apartment houses to those French readers who have never seen the US.

I should also add, to complete the impression, that one thinks at times, too, of the buildings put up for an exposition, but old, dirty ones, such as those that outlive by ten years the solemn occasion that brought them into being. For these shanties soon grow dirty, particularly in industrial areas.

Chicago, blackened by its smoke, made gloomy by the fogs of Lake Michigan, is a dark, grim red. Pittsburgh is even darker. And nothing is more striking at first than the contrast between the formidable power and inexhaustible abundance of what is called the 'American colossus' and the puny insignificance of the little houses that line the widest roads in the world. But, when one thinks of it, there is nothing that underlines better the fact that America is unfinished, that its ideas and plans, its social structure and cities have but a strictly provisional reality.

These cities laid out straight as a die bear not the slightest hint of organization. Many of them have the rudimentary structure of polyparies. Los Angeles, in particular, looks like a large earthworm you could cut into twenty sections without killing it. Moving through that enormous conurbation, which is probably the largest in the world, you come in succession to twenty juxtaposed cities, each strictly identical to the next, each with its poor district, its shopping streets, its nightclubs and its smart suburb; you get the impression that a medium-sized urban centre has made twenty copies of itself by scissiparous reproduction.[3]

This juxtaposition is the rule in America, where neighbourhoods are tacked on to each other as the prosperity of one region brings in new immigrants. You pass without transition from a poverty-stricken street to an aristocratic avenue. An esplanade lined with skyscrapers, museums and public monuments and adorned with lawns and trees comes to a sudden halt above a smoky station. And it is not unusual to find a wasteland of scrawny little kitchen gardens

---

3 To give the reader an idea of this city, I suggest he tries to imagine not one town on the Côte d'Azur, but the entire Côte d'Azur from Cannes to Menton.

beneath the tallest apartment blocks on some aristocratic avenue.

The fact is that the past, in these fast-moving cities—which are not built to grow old but which, like modern armies, advance by encircling islets of resistance they cannot destroy—does not manifest itself, as it does with us, in *monuments*, but in *survivals*. The wooden bridge in Chicago that crosses a canal a stone's throw from the world's highest skyscrapers is a survival. The elevated railways that rattle noisily through the streets of downtown Chicago and New York, supported by great iron pillars and cross-girders, almost touching the housefronts on either side, are survivals. They are quite simply there because there hasn't been time to pull them down; they are an indication of work still to be done.

The same disorder repeats itself in each individual vista. Nowhere else have I seen so many areas of wasteland. Admittedly, they have a precise function: they serve as car parks. But that doesn't mean they break up the alignment of the streets any less sharply. All of a sudden, it seems a bomb has dropped on three or four houses, reducing them to rubble, which has just been cleared away: this is a 'car park', two hundred square metres of bare earth with perhaps an advertising poster on a large hoarding as its sole ornamentation. Suddenly the city seems unfinished, badly put together. Equally suddenly, you are back in the desert and those great empty sites that were so striking at Fontana.

I recall the following landscape in Los Angeles: in the middle of the city two modern apartment blocks, two white cubes, frame an area of waste ground full of potholes—a car park. There are some automobiles parked there, seemingly abandoned. A palm tree grows like a weed between the cars. At the bottom, a steep grassy hill, somewhat akin to those mounds of our fortifications where we dump household waste. At the top of the mound, a wooden house. Not far below, a string is tied between two little trees, with multi-coloured washing hung out to dry on it. Walk around the blocks and the hill disappears; the other side of it has been faced with stone, asphalted and covered with tarmac roads; a magnificent tunnel runs through it.

What is particularly striking about American cities is the disorder in their height. The brick houses are of unequal size. A walk in Detroit produced the following succession, which I noted down randomly: one storey, two storeys, one storey, one storey, three storeys. You will find the same pattern at the other end of the country, in Albuquerque or San Antonio. Above and behind this irregular crenellation, you see buildings of all shapes and sizes: long, flat cases or fat, thirty-storey boxes of thirty or forty windows to a storey. As soon as there's a

little fog, the colours vanish. Volumes alone remain—
every variety of polyhedron. Between them lie enormous spaces, wastelands cut out of the sky.

In New York, and even in Chicago, the skyscraper
is on home ground. It imposes a new order on the city.
But everywhere else it is out of place. The eye can
establish no unity between these great beanpoles
and the little houses that run along the ground. It
searches, despite itself, for that skyline so well known
in European cities, but it cannot find it. This is why
the European initially has the sense of moving, not
through a city, but through a jumble of rocks that
looks like a city—not unlike Montpellier-le-Vieux.[4]

But he is also wrong to visit American cities the
way you visit Paris or Venice. They are not meant for
that. Streets here don't have the same meaning as they
do with us. In Europe, a street is halfway between a
major road and a covered 'public place'. It is on the
same level as the cafe, as is proved by the 'terraces' that
sprout on our pavements on fine days. So, its appear-
ance changes more than a hundred times a day, since
the crowd that throngs it changes and in Europe
human beings are its chief component. The American
street is a section of main road. It sometimes stretches

---

4 The rock labyrinth of Montpellier-le-Vieux near Millau
(Aveyron, France) is a series of strange rock formations that
looks in places like a ruined town. [Trans.]

over several miles. It does not encourage you to walk. Our streets are oblique and tortuous, full of recesses and secrets. The American street is a straight line; it yields itself immediately to the gaze and lacks mystery. Wherever you are, you can see from one end of it to the other. Moreover, in American cities the distances are too great to move around on foot. In most of them you travel almost exclusively by car, bus or subway train. Going from subway to escalator, escalator to taxi, taxi to bus and then again into the subway and a lift, I have sometimes travelled from one appointment to another like a parcel, never setting one foot in front of the other.

In some cities I found the pavements were genuinely atrophied. In Los Angeles, for example, on La Cinega, which is lined with bars, theatres, restaurants, antique shops and private residences, they are now scarcely more than the paths the guests and clients take to cross from the roadway into the building. Lawns have been laid between the facades and the roadway of this luxurious avenue. I followed a narrow path between these lawns for some time without encountering a living soul, while cars sped along the road to my right. All the animation of the street had found refuge on the roadway.

In New York and Chicago there are no neighbourhoods, but there is a neighbourhood life. The American does not know his city. Ten blocks from home, he is lost. This does not mean there are no crowds in the shopping streets. But it is a crowd that does not linger. People do their shopping or come out of the subway and go to their offices.

Only very rarely would I see a few Negroes daydreaming at a shop window.

Despite all this, you soon come to like American cities. Admittedly, they do all look alike. And it is disappointing to find, when you arrive in Wichita, St Louis, Albuquerque or Memphis, that hidden behind these magnificent, promising names is the same standard city with its checkerboard street pattern, the same red and green lights regulating the traffic and the same provincial air. But you gradually learn to tell one from the other. Chicago, noble and grim, red as the blood that streams through its slaughterhouses, with its canals, the grey water of Lake Michigan and its streets crushed between lumpish, mighty blocks is not a bit like San Francisco, that airy, briny city, sweeping down to the sea like an amphitheatre.

And then you end up liking their common element, the sense of the temporary. We are rather stifled in our fine, closed, chock-full cities. Our streets, winding and oblique, stumble into walls and houses. Once inside the city, you can no longer see beyond it. In America, these long straight unobstructed streets lead your gaze out of the city, as canals might do. Wherever you are, you see mountains or fields or the sea at the end of them.

Temporary and frail, formless and unfinished, these cities are haunted by the presence of the immense geographical space around them. Precisely because their boulevards are roads, they seem always to be staging-posts on a route. They are not oppressive, they never shut you in. Nothing in them is definitive or arrested. From the first glance, you feel your contact with these cities is a temporary one: either you will leave them or they will change around you.

But let us not exaggerate. In these same cities we have experienced American provincial Sundays—Sundays more oppressive than anywhere else on earth; we have seen the 'colonial style' suburban hostelries where, sitting in silence to the strains of an electric organ, middle-class families eat prawn cocktails and turkey in a sweet sauce at two dollars a head. We must not forget the dense layer of boredom that weighs upon America.

But these lightweight cities, still so like Fontana and the encampments of the Far West, show the other side of the US—its freedom. Everyone is free here, not to criticize or to reform how things are done, but to flee from it and go off into the desert or to some other town. The cities are open. They are open to the world and to the future. That is what gives them all an air of adventure; and, in their disorder and even ugliness, a kind of touching beauty.

Le Figaro (April 1945)

＊

NEW YORK, COLONIAL CITY

I knew I would love New York, but I thought I would be able to love it straight away, as I had loved the red bricks of Venice at first sight or the solid, sombre houses of London. I didn't know that for the European fresh off the plane, there is a 'New York sickness', akin to sea sickness, air sickness or altitude sickness.

An official coach had taken me from La Guardia airport to the Plaza Hotel at midnight. I had pressed my face against the window, but I could see only red and green lights and obscure buildings. The following day, without any transition, I found myself at the corner of Fifty-Eighth Street and Fifth Avenue. I took a long walk beneath an icy sky. It was a forlorn January Sunday in 1945 and I was looking for New York and couldn't find it. It was as though it drew back from me, like a ghost town, as I advanced along an avenue that seemed coldly mediocre and unoriginal. What I was looking for was, no doubt, a European city.

We Europeans live by the myth of the city we forged in the nineteenth century. The Americans' myths are not ours and the American city isn't our city. It hasn't the same nature or the same functions. In Spain, Italy, Germany or France, we find round cities originally encircled by ramparts, designed not only to protect the inhabitants from enemy invasion, but also to conceal from them the inexorable presence of nature. These cities are, moreover, divided into similarly rounded, closed districts. The tangle of jumbled houses weighs heavily on the ground. They seem to have a natural tendency to grow closer to each other— so much so that, from time to time, we have to take an axe to them to clear new paths, as you might in virgin forests. Streets run into other streets. They are closed at each end and do not seem to lead out of the city. Inside them, you go round in circles. They are more than mere arteries: each one is a social milieu. These are streets where you stop, meet people, drink, eat and linger. On Sundays, you dress up and take a stroll simply for the pleasure of greeting friends, of seeing and being seen. It is these streets that inspired Jules Romains' 'unanimism'. They are alive with a communal spirit that changes each hour of the day.

So, my short-sighted European eyes, venturing slowly and intently, strove in vain to find something to arrest them. Something, anything—a row of houses suddenly barring the way, a street corner or some old house bearing the patina of age. But to no avail. New York is a city for the long-sighted: you can 'focus' only at infinity. My gaze met nothing but space. It slid over blocks of identical houses, there being nothing to arrest it on its journey to the indistinctness of the horizon.

Céline called New York 'a vertical city'. This is true, but it seemed to me first a lengthways one. The traffic, at a standstill in the side streets, enjoys every possible privilege in the avenues, where it flows uninterrupted. How often the taxi-drivers, who are happy to take passengers north or south, refuse point blank to load up for east or west! The lateral streets have barely any other function than to mark the boundaries of the blocks between the avenues. The avenues cut through them and push them aside as they themselves rush on towards the north. It was for this reason, naive tourist that I was, that I looked long and fruitlessly for distinct 'neighbourhoods'. In France, our urban clusters surround and protect us. The rich neighbourhood protects the rich from the poor; the poor neighbourhood keeps us from the disdain of the rich; in the same way, the entire city protects us from nature.

In New York, where the main thoroughfares are parallel avenues, I was unable, except in Lower Broadway, to find neighbourhoods. I could find only atmospheres —gaseous masses stretching out longitudinally, with nothing to mark their beginning or their end. Gradually, I learned to recognize the atmosphere of Third Avenue, where, without even knowing each other, people meet, smile and chat in the shade of the noisy elevated railway; and that Irish bar where a German, passing by my table, stopped for a moment to say: 'You're French? I'm a Boche'; the reassuring comfort of the stores on Lexington Avenue; the staid elegance of Park Avenue; the cold luxury and stuccoed impassiveness of Fifth Avenue; the merry frivolity of Sixth and Seventh; the 'food fair' of Ninth and the no man's land of Tenth. Each avenue enwraps the neighbouring streets in its atmosphere, but a block away you suddenly plunge into another world. Not far from the thrilling silence of Park Avenue, home to the limousines of the powerful, I find myself on First Avenue, where the earth permanently shakes beneath the weight of passing trucks. How can I feel safe on one of these interminable north–south trajectories when, a few feet away to east or west, other longitudinal worlds lie in wait for me? Behind the Waldorf Astoria and the white and blue canopies of the 'elegant' buildings, I glimpse the 'Elevated', which carries with it something of the poverty of the Bowery.

The whole of New York is striped in this way with parallel, non-communicating meanings. These long lines, running straight as a die, suddenly gave me a sense of space. Our European cities are built to protect us against this: the houses cluster together there like sheep. But space runs through New York, animating and dilating it. Space, the great empty space of the steppes and the pampas, runs in its veins like a draught of cold air, separating those who live on the right from those who live on the left. In Boston, an American friend showing me round the smart neighbourhoods, pointed to the left of the street and said: 'This is where the "nice" people live.' And, pointing to the right, he added ironically, 'No one's ever found out who lives there.' It is the same in New York: between the two sides of a street, there is the whole of space.

New York is halfway between a city for pedestrians and a city for cars. You don't go for a walk in New York, you move through it; it is a city in motion. If I walk quickly, I feel at ease there. If I stop, I get flustered and wonder, 'Why am I on this street rather than on one of the hundreds of others like it?' Why in front of this drugstore, this branch of Schrafft's or Woolworth's, rather than any other one of the thousands like this?

And suddenly pure space appears. I imagine that a triangle, were it to acquire consciousness of its position in space, would be terror-stricken to learn of the rigour of its defining coordinates, and at the same time to discover that it is simply any old triangle, just anywhere. You never get lost in New York. You can see at a glance where you are: you are on the East Side, for example, at the corner of Fifty-Second Street and Lexington. But this spatial precision is not accompanied by any emotional exactitude. Amid the numerical anonymity of streets and avenues, I am simply anyone, anywhere. Wherever I am, my position is established in terms of longitude and latitude. But there is no valid reason to justify my presence at one spot rather than at another, since one place is so like another. I am never astray, but always lost.

Am I lost in a city or in nature? New York affords no protection from the violence of nature. It is a city open to the skies. The storms flood its streets that are so wide and take so long to cross when it rains. The hurricanes, announced solemnly on the radio like declarations of war, shake the brick houses and rock the skyscrapers. In summer, the air shimmers between the buildings. In winter, the city drowns as though you were in some Parisian suburb with the Seine overflowing, but here it is merely the snow melting.

Nature weighs so heavily on New York that this most modern of cities is also the dirtiest. From my window I can see the wind whipping up heavy muddy litter, which flits around on the pavement. Going out, I walk in blackish snow, a kind of puffy crust of the same hue as the sidewalk, as though that itself were buckling. From the end of May, the heat descends on the city like an atomic bomb. It is evil. People go up to each other and say: 'It's murder!' Millions of fleeing city-dwellers take to the trains, leaving damp marks on the seats when they get off, like snails. It isn't the city they are fleeing, but nature. Even in the depths of my apartment I suffer the depredations of a hostile, muffled, mysterious nature. I have the impression of camping in a jungle teeming with insects. There is the moaning of the wind, the electric shocks I get each time I touch a doorknob or shake a friend's hand, the cockroaches running round my kitchen, the elevators that make my stomach heave, the inextinguishable thirst that rages from morning to night. New York is a colonial city, a camp site. All the hostility and cruelty of nature are present in this city, the most prodigious monument humanity has ever raised to itself. It is a light city; its apparent weightlessness surprises most Europeans. In this immense, malevolent space, this desert of rock that brooks no vegetation, they have built thousands of houses out of brick, wood or rein-forced concrete, all of which seem about to fly away.

I love New York. I have learned to love it. I have got used to its massive clumps of buildings, its long vistas. My eyes no longer linger over the facades searching for one that might, by some remote chance, not be just like all the others. They rove immediately to the horizon, looking for blocks lost in fog, which are now mere volumes, merely the austere framing of the sky. When you know how to look at the two rows of buildings that line any major thoroughfare like cliffs, you get your reward: their mission is accomplished at the far end of the avenue in simple harmonious lines; a scrap of sky floats between them.

New York reveals itself only at a particular height, a particular distance, a particular speed. These are not the height, the distance or the speed of the pedestrian. The city is strikingly like the great Andalusian plains—monotonous when you pass through on foot, superb and varying when crossed by car.

I have learned to love its sky. In the low-roofed cities of Europe, the sky crawls along the ground and seems tamed. The beauty of the New York sky comes from its being raised so far above our heads by the skyscrapers. Pure and lonely as a wild beast, it mounts guard and stands watch over the city. And it isn't just a local protection: you feel that it stretches right out over the whole of America; it is the whole world's sky.

I have learned to love Manhattan's avenues. They are not sombre little walkways enclosed by houses, but national highways. As soon as you set foot in one of them you realize it has to go on as far as Boston or Chicago. Its vanishing point lies beyond the city and the eye can almost follow it out into the countryside. A wild sky above great parallel rails—that, first and foremost, is New York. In the heart of the city, you are in the heart of nature.

I had to get used to it, but now that I have, nowhere do I feel freer than amid the crowds of New York. This light, ephemeral city, which every morning and evening, beneath the curious rays of the sun, seems a mere juxtaposition of rectangular parallelepipeds, never oppresses or depresses. You can feel the anguish of solitude here, but not of prostration.

In Europe we cleave to a neighbourhood, a block of houses or a street corner, and we are no longer free. But hardly have you plunged into New York than you live entirely on its scale. You can look over it in the evening from up on the Queensboro Bridge, in the morning from New Jersey or at noon from the seventy-seventh floor of the Rockefeller Center, but you will never be captivated by any of its streets because none has a distinctive beauty all its own. Beauty is present in each of them, just as nature and the sky of the whole of America are present in them. Nowhere will you form a better sense of the simultaneity of human lives.

New York moves us Europeans despite its austerity. We have, admittedly, learned to love our old cities, but what touches us in them is a Roman wall forming part of the facade of an inn, a house where Cervantes lived, the Place des Vosges or the town hall at Rouen. We love museum-cities—and all our cities are a little like museums where we wander amid our ancestors' dwellings. New York isn't a museum-city. Yet for Frenchmen of my generation it already possesses the melancholy of the past. When we were twenty—around 1925—we heard about the skyscrapers. For us they symbolized the fabulous prosperity of America. We discovered them with stupefaction in the movies. They were the architecture of the future, just as cinema was the art of the future and jazz the music of the future. Today we know all about jazz: it is more a music of the past than of the future. It is a popular black music, capable of limited development, but in gentle decline. It has had its day. And the talkies have not fulfilled the promise of the silents: Hollywood moulders on in a rut.

The war clearly revealed to the Americans that America is the world's greatest power. But the age of easy living is over: many economists fear a new recession. Hence, no skyscrapers are being built now. It seems they are too difficult to let.

To the man who strolled through New York before 1930, the high-rise buildings towering over the city were the first signs of an architecture destined to radiate over the entire country. Skyscrapers then were living things. Today, for a Frenchman arriving from Europe, they are already mere historical monuments, witnesses to a bygone age. They still rise up into the sky but my spirit does not soar with them, and the

New Yorkers pass by at their feet without so much as a glance. I cannot think of them without melancholy: they speak of an age when we thought the war to end; war had just finished, an age when we believed in peace. They are already a little run-down: tomorrow, perhaps, they will be demolished. At any rate, to build them took a faith we no longer possess.

I walk between little brick houses the colour of dried blood. They are younger than Europe's houses, but their fragility makes them seem much older. I see in the distance the Empire State and Chrysler Buildings pointing vainly to the sky and it suddenly occurs to me that New York is on the point of acquiring a history and that it already has its ruins.

That is enough to soften somewhat the edges of the harshest city in the world.

Town and Country (May 1946)

＊

Everything has been said about the US. But once a person has crossed the Atlantic he can no longer be satisfied with even the most perceptive of books. Not that he doesn't believe their message. But his commitment to it remains abstract. When a friend claims to explain our character and fathom our intentions, when he relates each of our actions to principles, prejudices, beliefs and a worldview that are, in his view, our own, we hear him out uneasily, without being able to either deny what he says or entirely accept it. Perhaps the construction is true, but true in what sense? The intimate warmth, the life, is lacking, as is that unpredictability one always represents for oneself and that weary familiarity also, and that decision to come to terms with—or run from—oneself and the endless deliberations and the perpetual invention of what one is, and the vow to be *this* and not something else: in a word, freedom.

In a similar way, when we in Europe are presented with a careful arrangement of the notions of melting-pot, puritanism, realism, optimism, etc., which we are told are the key to the American character, we feel a certain intellectual satisfaction and believe that it must indeed be that way. But when we walk in New York on Third, Sixth or Tenth Avenue at that hour of the evening that Leonardo saw as lending greater gentleness to the human countenance, we encounter the most moving faces in the world, faces uncertain and questing, assiduous, full of a wide-eyed good faith, with eyes that call out to us, and we know that the finest constructions will be of little use. They will enable us to understand the system, but not the people.

The system is a great external apparatus, an implacable machine we might call the objective spirit of the US and which, over there, they call 'Americanism'. It is a complex monster of myths, values, recipes, slogans, figures and rites. But we should not believe it has been deposited in the head of every American the way Descartes' God deposited his primary notions in the human mind. We should not believe it is 'refracted' into brains and hearts, at every moment determining affections or thoughts that are its rigorous expression. It is, in fact, outside them; it is *presented* to the citizens. The cleverest propaganda presents it to them incessantly, but it only ever presents it to them: it is not *it* that is in *them*, but *they* who are in *it*. They battle against it or accept it; they stifle in it or transcend it; they suffer it or repeatedly reinvent it anew; they give in to it or make furious efforts to escape it. In any event, *it* remains external to them, transcendent, for they are human beings and *it* is a thing.

There are the great myths—the myths of happiness, progress, freedom and triumphant motherhood—the realism and the optimism; and then there are the Americans who are nothing at first, who grow up between these colossal statues and make out as best they can amongst them. There is the myth of happiness; there are these bewitching slogans that tell you to be happy as quickly as possible; there are the films with 'happy endings' which, every evening, present exhaus-ted crowds with a rose-tinted view of life; there is that language loaded with optimistic, carefree expressions—'have a good time', 'enjoy', 'life is fun', etc. And then there are these people who are haunted, even in the most conformist bliss, by an obscure, nameless malaise, these people who are tragic for fear of being so, from that total absence of the tragic in them and around them.

There is this community that prides itself on being the least 'historic' in the world; on never complicating its problems with inherited custom and acquired rights; on facing up, as a blank sheet, to a blank future where anything is possible. And then there are the blind stumblings of so many lost sheep who are trying to find sustenance in a tradition, a folklore. There are those films that write American history for the masses and which, for want of being able to serve up a Kentucky Joan of Arc or a Kansas Charlemagne, thrill those masses with the story of Al Jolson, jazz singer, or the composer George Gershwin. There is the Monroe Doctrine, isolationism and the contempt for Europe. And then there is every American's sentimental attachment to his country of origin and the intellectuals' inferiority complex towards the culture of the old Continent: the critics who say, 'How can you admire our novelists when you have Flaubert?' and the painters who say, 'I'll never be able to paint so long as I stay in the US.' There is the slow, barely perceptible effort of a whole nation to seize hold of universal history and assimilate it as its heritage. There is the myth of equality and there is 'segregation' and those great hotels in the Atlantic beach resorts with signs outside saying 'No Jews and no dogs', the Connecticut lakes where Jews are forbidden to bathe and the table of racial ranks where the lowest place is assigned to the Slavs and the highest to the Dutch immigrants who go back to 1680. There is the myth of freedom and the dictatorship of public opinion, the myth of economic liberalism and those big companies that extend over a whole continent which ultimately belong to no one and where everyone, from top to bottom, works like a functionary in a state industry. There is the legalistic mania that leads each citizen to call for new laws at every turn and the secret anarchy, that 'law of the heart', that leads them to find a loophole in every one. There is the smiling belief in progress and the deep discouragement and pessimism of the intellectuals, who think that action is impossible. There is the respect for science and industry, the positivism, the fanatical love of gadgetry, and there is the dark humour of the *New Yorker* that bitterly mocks mechanical civilization and those hundred million Americans who beguile their immense need for the fantastic by reading the improbable adventures of Superman, Wonderwoman and Mandrake the Magician in the comic books.

There are the thousand taboos proscribing sex outside marriage, and then there are the carpets of used condoms in the backyards of the co-ed colleges, the cars parked by the road sides every evening with their lights off, all the men and women who drink before making love, so that they can sin while drunk and not remember it. There are the neat, tidy houses, the apartments all done out in white, with radio, rocking chair and pipe in the pipe box—veritable paradises. And then there are the tenants of these apartments who, after dinner, walk out on rocking chair, radio, wife, pipe and children and drink themselves into a stupor alone in the bar opposite. Perhaps nowhere will you find such a discrepancy between men and myths, between life and the collective representation of life. An American once said to me in Berne, 'The truth is that each of us has a nagging fear of being less American than his neighbour.' I accept this explanation. It shows that Americanism isn't a mere myth dinned into people's heads by artful propaganda, but that every American tentatively reinvents it at every moment, that it is both a grand external form, which stands at the entry to the port of New York, opposite the Statue of Liberty, and the daily product of uneasy freedoms. There is a sense of anxiety about Americanism in the American; there is an ambivalence to his anxiety, as though he were asking himself both: 'Am I American enough?' and 'How can I escape Americanism?' A human being in America is a certain simultaneous answer to these two questions; and each human being must find his answers alone.

The reader will be very disappointed if he expects to find an exhaustive study of America's problems here.[1] There is no point my saying what is lacking: in a sense, almost everything. But our aim has been to show human beings. Of all these articles, only six were written by Europeans; only six present the situation 'objectively'. In all the others, the authors speak of

---

1 This piece was written as an introduction to an issue of *Les Temps modernes* on America. [Trans.]

themselves and their condition: it is blacks who write about the Negroes,[2] an American psychoanalyst who writes about psychoanalysis, a New Yorker who writes of Broadway and the life story of Mrs Gertrude R. is told by that lady's very own daughter. So each of these testimonies is impassioned: Wylie's 'Mom' is an explosion of rage; we do not publish it with any documentary intent, but as typical of certain violent—and unjust—reactions of Americans to their own myths. They are also acts: 'Black Metropolis' isn't comparable to the studies of USA's Negro problem by Myrdal, the European; it is an attempt by intelligent, educated Negroes to raise the level of their race. The presentation of Negro spirituals is made by a great black poet who wants to demonstrate to whites the originality of Negro music. Greenberg's article on American art is an episode in a battle he is fighting against a certain form of painting and aesthetic. All these people feel intimately bound up with what they are condemning or approving. It is themselves they are scourging or caressing. And don't think that any of them feels he is *doing* America *down* (with the exception, perhaps, of Wylie, though even then it is not certain). For a Frenchman, to expose an abuse is to do France down, because he sees the country in the past tense and as unchangeable. For an American, to do so is to pave

2 To avoid anachronism, the term 'nègre' has been translated as 'Negro' throughout. [Trans.]

the way for reform, as he sees his country in the future tense. When Greenberg writes that, in the US, art is left to 'the semi-educated, the gullible, the spinsters and the outmoded visionaries', you can be sure he regards this as a temporary state of affairs. These writers all take the view that America is as yet unfinished; they all write their articles from the standpoint of the future. It is these people we wanted to present, with their faith, their fury, their sense of passionate injustice, their lucidity too; with their goodwill, their way of judging and, at the same time, of *making* America. Each of these articles seems to me to be a face. A worried face, a face of stirring liberty. And it is precisely this we want to proffer to those readers who have not crossed the Atlantic and who do not yet know the strange, weary softness faces assume when the first lights are coming on on Broadway.

Les Temps modernes (August 1946)

＊

A NOTE ON SOURCES

'The Republic of Silence'

Originally published as 'La République du Silence' in *Situations III*, NEW EDN (Paris: Gallimard, 2003), pp. 11–14.

First published in English translation in *The Aftermath of War* (London: Seagull Books, 2008), pp. 3–7.

'Paris under the Occupation'

Originally published as 'Paris sous l'Occupation' in *Situations III*, NEW EDN (Paris: Gallimard, 2003), pp. 15–34.

First published in English translation in *The Aftermath of War* (London: Seagull Books, 2008), pp. 8–40.

'What is a Collaborator?'

Originally published as 'Qu'est-ce qu'un collaborateur' in *Situations III*, NEW EDN (Paris: Gallimard, 2003), pp. 35–48.

First published in English translation in *The Aftermath of War* (London: Seagull Books, 2008), pp. 41–64.

'The End of the War'

Originally published as 'La fin de la guerre' in *Situations III*, NEW EDN (Paris: Gallimard, 2003), pp. 49–58.

First published in English translation in *The Aftermath of War* (London: Seagull Books, 2008), pp. 65–78.

'Individualism and Conformism in the United States'

Originally published as 'Individualisme et conformisme aux États-Unis' in *Situations III*, NEW EDN (Paris: Gallimard, 2003), pp. 59–70.

First published in English translation in *The Aftermath of War* (London: Seagull Books, 2008), pp. 81–99.

'Cities of America'

Originally published as 'Villes d'Amérique' in *Situations III*, NEW EDN (Paris: Gallimard, 2003), pp. 71–84.

First published in English translation in *The Aftermath of War* (London: Seagull Books, 2008), pp. 100–120.

'New York, Colonial City'

Originally published as 'New York, ville coloniale' in *Situations III*, NEW EDN (Paris: Gallimard, 2003), pp. 85–94.

First published in English translation in *The Aftermath of War* (London: Seagull Books, 2008), pp. 121–33.

'USA: Presentation'

Originally published as 'U.S.A. Présentation' in *Situations III*, NEW EDN (Paris: Gallimard, 2003), pp. 95–102.

First published in English translation in *The Aftermath of War* (London: Seagull Books, 2008), pp. 134–44.